BUILDING A QUALITY
TEACHING FORCE

BUILDING A QUALITY TEACHING FORCE

Lessons Learned from Alternate Routes

Edited by

C. Emily Feistritzer

National Center for Education Information
National Center for Alternative Certification

PEARSON

Merrill
Prentice Hall

Upper Saddle River, New Jersey
Columbus, Ohio

Library of Congress Cataloging-in-Publication Data

Building a quality teaching force : lessons learned from alternate routes /
  [edited by] C. Emily Feistritzer.
    p. cm.
  Includes bibliographical references and index.
  ISBN-13: 978-0-13-238212-0 (pbk.)
  ISBN-10: 0-13-238212-1 (pbk.)
    1. Teachers—Training of—United States.   2. Teachers—Recruiting—United
States.   3. Teachers—Certification—United States.   4. Alternative
education—United States.   I. Feistritzer, C. Emily.
  LB1715.B82 2008
  331.7'611371100973—dc22

                                                                2007013668

Vice President and Executive Publisher: Jeffery W. Johnston
Senior Editor: Darcy Betts Prybella
Project Manager: Kris Roach
Production Coordination: Thistle Hill Publishing Services, LLC
Design Coordinator: Diane C. Lorenzo
Cover Designer: Jason Moore
Cover Image: SuperStock
Production Manager: Susan Hannahs
Director of Marketing: David Gesell
Marketing Coordinator: Brian Mounts

This book was set in NewBaskerville by Integra Software Services. It was printed
and bound by Courier Stoughton. The cover was printed by Courier Stoughton.

Pearson Education Ltd.   Pearson Education Australia Pty. Limited
Pearson Education Singapore Pte. Ltd.   Pearson Education North Asia Ltd.
Pearson Education Canada, Ltd.   Pearson Educación de Mexico, S.A. de C.V.
Pearson Education–Japan   Pearson Education Malaysia Pte. Ltd.

10 9 8 7 6 5 4 3 2 1
ISBN-13: 978-0-13-238212-0
ISBN-10:   0-13-238212-1

PREFACE

Building a quality teaching force has been a focus of the nation since the first schoolhouses were built in Jamestown. Numerous approaches have been proposed and implemented—from raising pay for teachers to improving working conditions to a myriad of recommendations that have dealt with aspects of teacher preparation through undergraduate and graduate college programs. Such programs still play a role in teacher preparation; but significant new developments have occurred that are having a profound impact on numerous aspects of the teaching profession—all leading to building a truly high-quality teaching force. Since the mid-1980s, alternative routes to teaching have not only grown and developed, they have dramatically affected almost every aspect of teaching in the United States such as:

- Who enters teaching
- How individuals are recruited, selected, and placed in teaching jobs
- Criteria for entry into teaching
- Preparation for teaching
- Certification of teachers

Since the mid-1980s, when New Jersey, California, and Texas created the first alternate routes to teaching designed specifically to attract and accommodate the needs of a new market for teaching—individuals who already had at least a bachelor's degree—every state in the nation now has at least one alternate route to teacher certification. As of 2006, 130 alternate routes to certification had been established by the states and were being implemented in at least 485 programs which produced some 59,000 new teachers—one-third of all new teachers hired in 2006–2007. Data from the states indicate that these programs are very effective in accomplishing the following:

- Meeting the demand efficiently and effectively for highly qualified teachers in the areas where demand is greatest
- Producing teachers who are committed to teaching and stay in the jobs for which they were recruited and in which they were trained
- Screening and selecting teachers competent to teach the subjects and grade levels they teach, resulting in noticeable student achievement gains

This book presents the evidence gleaned from people who have been at the forefront of working with alternate route programs. The authors describe lessons learned in key areas of demonstrated success in building a quality teaching force through alternate routes to teaching:

- Recruitment and selection of candidates for successful teaching
- Mentoring and support
- Program content and curriculum
- Candidate assessment
- Organization and management

The book is designed to assist those creating and/or implementing programs for the preparation of teachers primarily in field-based settings. Chapter 1 provides a summary and overview of the alternate routes to teacher certification movement. A complete description of alternate routes can be found in the companion book, *Alternate Routes to Teaching*, by C. Emily Feistritzer and Charlene K. Haar, also published by Pearson/Prentice Hall.

Michelle Rhee, the founder, president, and CEO of The New Teacher Project (TNTP), has developed a highly successful recruitment, selection, and placement program that is being implemented throughout the United States. The profound lessons learned from that program in contributing to building a quality teaching force are explained in Chapter 2, which she co-authors with David Keeling.

Mentoring and induction are now identified as essential to the success of any new beginning teacher. Mentoring has been an essential component of alternate routes since their inception. Ellen Moir of the New Teacher Center at Santa Cruz is considered the nation's premier expert in this area. Moir has designed and is implementing mentor and induction training in schools and school districts throughout the nation. In Chapter 3, she shares what the New Teacher Center has learned and is doing in this critical area of ensuring that teachers gain the competence to be effective teachers.

The question of what every teacher should know and be able to teach is an age-old problem in education. In Chapter 4, Becky Washington, director of the highly regarded Texas Region XIII alternate route program, which was featured as one of six exemplary alternate route programs in the U.S. Department of Education's *Innovations in Education: Alternative Routes to Teacher Certification (2004)*, has tackled this question and created a content and curriculum framework that attempts to answer the questions concerning content and curriculum.

Assessment of teacher competence and effectiveness is a critical variable in determining the success of any teacher preparation program. Eileen McDaniel, senior educational program director for communication and policy development, Bureau of Educator Certification at the Florida Department of Education, and Karen Wilde, previously the program director of the Florida Department of Education's Bureau of Educator Certification, tackle this issue and provide a road map for effective candidate assessment in Chapter 5.

Michael McKibbin has been involved in teacher education and certification throughout his career. For the past 22 years, he has worked for the State of California and is currently working in program evaluation and research for the California Commission on Teacher Credentialing. McKibbin has been intimately involved in alternate routes to certification, not only in California but across the nation, since they began in the early 1980s. He is well positioned to reflect on this movement. His valuable insights into what works and what doesn't and the management of programs, goal setting, and program implementation are discussed in Chapter 6.

Alternate routes to teacher certification are part of an evolutionary process to ensure that the nation builds a quality teaching force. Since their controversial beginnings in the early 1980s, alternate routes have had—and continue to have—a significant impact on who enters teaching, when and how they enter the profession, what and where they teach, and how they become effective teachers. Lessons learned from these alternate routes in building a quality teaching force are the subject of this book. The information shared by the authors—all of whom have been in the trenches, as it were, in building a quality teaching force—is meant not only to educate but also to be implemented in all programs for the preparation of teachers.

ACKNOWLEDGMENTS

This book is the result of a true collaboration of efforts of a major publishing company that recognized the growing role of alternate routes to teaching and individuals who had been actively involved in them for a very long time. It has been an exciting ride from when Pearson first contacted me two years ago to the publication of this book, as well as *Alternate Routes to Teaching* (© 2008) and the upcoming series for candidates in teacher preparation programs. These are important works and could not have been done without the authors of each of the chapters of this book—Michelle Rhee and David Keeling; Ellen Moir; Becky Washington; Eileen McDaniel and Karen Wilde; and Michael McKibbin. Their tireless attention to this project through several transitions resulted in a truly informative and useful book. I am indebted to them and to the many people at Pearson Education, from Jeff Johnston, publisher of the Merrill/Prentice Hall imprint of Pearson, and Kevin Johnson, who started it all; to Debbie Stollenwerk, our first executive editor to Darcy Betts, the current senior editor.

In addition, I thank the following reviewers for providing valuable feedback in the final stages of manuscript preparation: Catherine Cormany, Pennsylvania Department of Education; Colleen Finegan, Wright State University; and Robert Lucking, Old Dominion University.

Lastly, I wish to thank Charlene Haar, my colleague and friend, whose attention to detail contributed so much to this project.

C. Emily Feistritzer
Editor

BRIEF CONTENTS

CONTENTS

Note: Every effort has been made to provide accurate and current Internet information in this book. However, the Internet and information on it are constantly changing, so it is inevitable that some of the Internet addresses listed in this textbook will change.

1

Introduction and Overview

C. Emily Feistritzer

*A*lternative routes to teaching are having a major impact on the teaching profession in the United States, affecting not only the number of individuals entering teaching but who enters teaching, how, and why. In 2006, approximately a third of the 147,000 new-to-the-profession teachers hired by school districts came through alternative routes to teacher certification.[1] Alternative routes to teacher certification are state-approved nontraditional routes that permit teacher candidates who already have at least a bachelor's degree to enter classrooms and obtain teacher certification in an expedited manner.

Although it began in a handful of states in the mid-1980s amid much furor and fanfare,[2] alternative routes to teaching have proliferated at a rapid rate. As of 2007, every state in the United States was implementing at least one alternate route to teacher certification, up from just eight states in 1983. In some states, 30% to 40% of all new teachers hired are from alternate route programs. In 2007, 130 alternative routes to teacher certification were implemented in approximately 500 alternate route programs that produced approximately 60,000 new teachers.

In the 1980s, the developments of alternate routes were characterized by two rather divergent phenomena:

1. A focus in a few states to develop new and different ways of recruiting nontraditional candidates for teaching and the creation of new pathways for certifying them to teach.

---

[1]Statistics used throughout this chapter are from data collected by the National Center for Education Information and published in *Alternative Teacher Certification: A State-by-State Analysis 2007, Profile of Alternate Route Teachers 2005, Profile of Teachers in the U.S. 2005,* and on the Website www.teach-now.org.
[2]For a thorough discussion of the development of alternate routes, see Feistritzer and Haar, *Alternate Routes to Teaching, 2007.*

2. A flurry in several states to rename as "alternate routes" existing teacher certification routes, such as emergency or other forms of temporary certificates.

The early to late 1990s saw some real definitions emerge about what was and what was not an alternate route to teacher certification. More and more states not only stopped calling their emergency and temporary certificates "alternate routes," they dropped these designations altogether.

By the late 1990s, as the states developed and approved alternate routes, common characteristics of alternate routes and alternate route programs began to emerge:

- States designed alternate routes specifically to recruit, prepare, and license talented individuals who already had at least a bachelor's degree, who often had careers in fields other than education, but who had decided to change careers and begin to teach.
- Alternate route programs implemented rigorous screening processes, such as passing tests, interviews, and demonstrated mastery of subject-matter content.
- Alternate route programs included on-the-job training (field-based programs) that included working with mentor teachers and/or other support personnel.
- Alternate route programs included coursework or equivalent experiences in professional education studies before and while teaching.
- Alternate route programs maintained high performance standards for completion of the programs.

Those common characteristics are still part of exemplary alternate route programs. In 2006, colleges and universities administered nearly half (46%) of the new alternate route programs. The growing community college market administered an additional 6% of alternate route programs. Twenty-four percent of alternate routes leading to teacher certification are administered by school districts. The operative term is *administered by*. Nearly every alternative route to teacher certification is, in fact, collaboration among the state licensing authority, institutions of higher education, and local school districts.

In addition to increasing the number of individuals being prepared to teach, alternate routes are affecting other aspects of teaching:

1. Who enters teaching
2. How supply and demand provide opportunities for teaching
3. How teachers are prepared through on-the-job training, certified, and placed in jobs
4. How long teachers stay in the profession

About half of the teachers who have entered through alternate routes say they would not have become teachers if the alternate route had not existed.

Because alternate routes exist for the purpose of transitioning individuals into teaching who already have at least a bachelor's degree, opportunities are available to many individuals who can add to the demographic mix of the existing teacher workforce. Although the overall teaching force is only 15% nonwhite, a third of teachers entering through alternate routes are nonwhite. Four out of 10 individuals entering teaching through alternate routes are 40 years of age or older. Alternate routes attract more men, who are 37% of alternate route teachers, compared to 18% of the overall teaching force.

About half of the approximately 50,000 individuals who entered teaching through alternate routes in 2006 came into teaching from a field other than education. Only a fifth of alternate route teachers had prior experience in an education field, such as a substitute teacher, part-time teacher, or teacher aide. To meet the needs of mature adults coming from other careers, alternate route programs create content and curriculum targeted to these individuals, many of whom have considerable life experiences beneficial to the classroom.

As a market-driven phenomenon, alternate routes recruit, select, and train individuals for specific jobs in specific subject areas in specific geographic areas where demand for teachers is greatest. Often the demand for teachers is greatest in urban and rural areas and in subjects such as mathematics, science, and special education. Nearly all (97%) of the providers of alternate route programs say their teachers serve students in a high-need area (e.g., low socioeconomic area, high poverty level, and high minority) school.

Alternate route programs are flexible enough to train individuals to teach the high-demand subjects in high-need schools. Teacher shortages are being alleviated through market-driven alternate routes, especially in the high-demand subject areas. Twenty percent of alternate route teachers teach mathematics, compared with 7% of all teachers. Similarly, more than half of alternate route teachers are trained as special education teachers, compared with 38% of all teachers.

Nearly all alternate route programs involve on-the-job training, with candidates starting out as teachers of record and receiving salaries and benefits—a critical component for career switchers.

Data from providers of alternate route programs show that nearly all of those who complete an alternate route program and receive a teaching certificate are teaching the following year, usually in the same school where they taught while in the program. Furthermore, a high percentage of teachers (85% to 90% in most states that have active alternate routes) who enter the profession through alternate routes are still teaching 5 years later. This is significantly higher than teachers prepared through the traditional college campus-based teacher education programs; only half are still teaching 5 years after beginning their first teaching job.

The age-old questions of "What does every teacher need to know and be able to do? And how can we assess whether or not a prospective teacher knows and can do those things?" form the bases on which alternate route programs have been developed. As just noted, alternate route programs are designed to meet the needs of a more mature, diverse, and career/life-experienced cadre of adults who want to teach. And those who want to teach often want to do so in high-need schools near where the individuals already reside. Teacher candidates in an alternative route program earn a salary while they learn to teach, another important component of the impact of alternate routes.

Of the hundreds of alternate route programs, many share similar characteristics, but many also have adopted a variety of unique strategies and requirements. The following chapters highlight some of those exemplary programs and practices that have proven to be very effective in the development and implementation of alternate route programs. In fact, development of alternative routes has highlighted the importance of these practices in ensuring that teachers are indeed qualified. For example, the emphasis on recruiting from a wide selection of candidates and careful and purposeful selection of teacher candidates is a hallmark of effective alternative certification programs.

Similarly, the concept of mentoring beginning teachers in alternate route programs has had a profound impact from statehouses to schoolhouses. As mentoring techniques become standardized, the effects have become increasingly valuable for beginning teachers—and even for those who serve as mentors.

The authors who write about the significance of these processes are practitioners who have "been there and done that" and have become experts in the field. In both general and specific ways, the suggestions by the authors may help others in the development or improvement of not only alternate route programs, but all programs for the preparation of teachers.

The chapters in this book are organized as a program profile, beginning with recruitment and selection of candidates.

The authors of Chapter 2, Michelle Rhee and David Keeling, are recognized experts in the recruitment and selection of teacher candidates to alternate route programs. Rhee serves as chief executive officer and president of The New Teacher Project (TNTP). TNTP is a nonprofit organization that partners with school districts, state departments of education, and other educational entities to enhance their capacity to recruit, select, train, and support outstanding new teachers for hard-to-staff schools.

Since its inception in 1997, TNTP has launched more than 40 programs in 22 states and attracted and prepared over 15,000 new high-quality teachers hired through TNTP's alternate route to certification programs for school districts in New York City, Washington, D.C., Los Angeles, Atlanta, Baltimore, and other cities.

From its experiences, TNTP has identified three challenges that face a school district in meeting its professional personnel needs: (1) unfocused recruitment strategies, (2) flawed application and hiring processes, and (3) inconsistent selection practices. Rhee and Keeling describe each of these recruitment and hiring challenges, pointing out how missteps can contribute to consistently overlooking candidates who would make effective, dedicated teachers.

The solution offered by TNTP is its research-based selection model to evaluate objectively each applicant's core characteristics and abilities. By using a hypothetical alternate route program, TNTP offers a proven path with standardized requirements to successful recruitment and selection of teacher candidates. Quality control, careful thinking, data tracking, and systematic evaluation are all necessary components, as are time, money, and the right people to implement the model.

"These strategies work," write the authors. "Reliable data, compelling messages, customer service, and accurate selection tools matter not for their own sake, but because of how much rides on their collective contribution to the program's overall success: the quality of the teachers it produces and the future of the students who sit in their classrooms."

Rhee's commitment to excellence in education began in 1992 when she started her teaching career at Harlem Park Community School in Baltimore, Maryland, as part of the Teach For America program. Her outstanding successes in the classroom and as the founder of TNTP have earned her acclaim and extensive media coverage.

Chapter 3 continues the progression of developing a profile of the components of an exemplary alternate route program. Chapter author Ellen Moir is the founder and executive director of the New Teacher Center at the University of California, Santa Cruz. For more than 20 years, Ellen Moir has pioneered innovative approaches to new teacher development, research on new teacher practice, and the design and administration of teacher induction programs.

Moir writes, "An effective induction program includes professional development for both the novice teacher and the mentor, and training that will make reflection and assessment an ongoing component of the teacher's professional practice." Before that could happen, teachers had to remain on the job.

Moir provides the historical context in California when the state faced exceptionally low rates of teacher retention because when teachers entered the classroom, they were left to "sink or swim." The state legislature stepped in with funding, and eventually a diverse partnership of education officials and the University of Santa Cruz established mentor-based programs throughout the state.

To illustrate the significance of how a mentor's wise and trusted counsel can be effective to a beginning teacher, the author carefully details the key criteria for successful induction of a beginning teacher, starting with the selection of a mentor. Mentors who are the most effective, writes Moir, "have keen observational proficiency, excellent communication skills, and, of course, patience, enthusiasm, and a love of all kinds of learning."

Since 1988, the Santa Cruz New Teacher Project has worked with over 9,000 K–12 new teachers in California. To give national scope to its successful induction/mentor work in California, the University of California Santa Cruz, Moir, and others established the New Teacher Center (NTC). The NTC now collaborates with school districts in several states to provide professional development training for mentors. Although the NTC has its own proprietary training modules, you can gain insights from the topics of the training as well as the sequence of the topics for the recommended 2-year training for mentors. The author provides a complete picture of the key components of an effective program—how to begin, how to create stakeholder buy-in of the critical components, and how to improve the program through assessments. Moir writes, "[the] benefits reflect the fact that mentoring transforms the teaching profession from an atmosphere of isolation and high turnover to one of collaboration, continuity, and community."

As senior coordinator of the educator certification program at the Region XIII Education Service Center in Austin, Texas, Becky Washington has developed a curriculum. In 2004, the U.S. Department of Education selected the Region XIII alternate route program as one of six exemplary programs in the United States, in part because of its strong mentor support and tailored field-based programming.

In Chapter 4, Washington takes you through steps to design a curriculum to develop quality teachers. Region XIII built a curriculum program around standards using the *backward-design approach*. This is one of many excellent curriculum development approaches used in alternate routes.

Region XIII designed its program curriculum, starting from what the candidates would need to know and be able to do based on the state requirements and standards. State requirements include those necessary for the credential itself, established by the State Board for Educator Certification and aligned with state board exams. The state Professional Development and Appraisal System Framework sets the standards for the teaching profession, and the Texas Essential Knowledge and Skills (TEKS) covers the standards that drive the academic content encountered by K–12 students.

Based on those criteria, Region XIII staff then determined what evidence candidates would have to produce to demonstrate having met the state standards. Finally, Region XIII developed the learning activities intended to enable candidates to generate that evidence.

The resulting curriculum requires preservice training for the elementary, special education, and bilingual candidates with online coursework to address the "highly qualified" component of the *No Child Left Behind* legislation. After completion, candidates in these areas must pass a content examination. Region XIII requires all teacher candidates to take the following courses:

- Learning Foundations (human growth, development, and learning theory)
- Lesson Design (lesson cycles and how to incorporate standards into lessons)
- Classroom Environment (how to establish a positive environment)
- The "Learner" (instructional and questioning strategies)
- Beyond the "Learner" (designed to help the candidate develop a strong philosophy regarding being an educator)

At the end of the program, Region XIII surveys its candidates on a wide range of issues. Questions cover the program's overall performance, the quality of the training, the caliber of support from mentors and supervisors, and candidates' expectations for the future. Continuous program improvement depends on committed, collaborative leadership and inclusive decision making. At an annual retreat, Region XIII staff analyze all survey data collected. Washington writes of the 15-member full-time staff, saying, "they pride themselves on being able to 'turn on a dime' to make changes."

Furthermore, Washington reports that "this process leads to developing teachers who begin their first year of teaching with the knowledge and skills needed to positively impact the achievement of their students."

The Region XIII Education Service Center serves the 16-county Austin area and is one of 20 such agencies created by the Texas legislature to function as intermediaries between the Texas Education Agency and local school districts. Critical teacher shortages for the 59 school districts in and around Austin, Texas, stimulated the state to create this alternate route program in 1989.

Authors Eileen McDaniel and Karen Wilde start out Chapter 5 with a quotation from *Alice in Wonderland:* "If you don't know where you're going, any place will do." McDaniel and Wilde write that "investing the energy and resources needed to create an alternative teacher certification program will not lead to the goal of successful student learning without the guidance of a map." The map, the authors say, is "a solid candidate assessment system that defines each program's destination."

Throughout Chapter 5, authors McDaniel and Wilde take you through candidate assessment, one of the 12 competencies or practices adopted by Florida that define an alternate route program's destination. The Florida Educator Accomplished Practices (FEAP) "are for teachers what Florida's 'Sunshine State Standards' are for students," they write.

A sound system for assessing candidates must be valid, reliable, and fair. To be valid, assessment techniques must measure specific performance or behaviors that can be demonstrated by the teacher as reflective of the standard against which the measurement is taken. Reliability is the degree to which the assessment tasks are free from measurement errors. And a fair assessment system includes a system that is free of bias or discrimination that could have adverse effects on certain populations.

Next, in keeping with their road map analogy, the authors point out the signs or markers that guide the developing teacher in knowing precisely what outcomes are expected. A trained assessor uses precise criteria to determine if each classroom product, for example pre- and posttests, is linked to student achievement. In Florida, the assessor determines if each task and/or product completed is "acceptable," "marginal," or "unacceptable." In addition, the assessor determines the level of the candidate's overall performance as "demonstrated," indicating that 67% of the individual task criteria are acceptable and none unacceptable; "partially demonstrated," indicating that less than 67% of the individual task criteria are acceptable and none are unacceptable; or "not demonstrated," if one or more criteria are rated as "unacceptable."

Finally, the assessor must determine if the candidate's overall performance throughout all 12 practices (competencies) meets the requirements for certification. Again, FEAP allows the assessor to produce a cumulative score to indicate the candidate is "accomplished," "competent," or "not competent" based on specific criteria. The authors write that "*all* 12 teacher practices are equally critical to effective teaching that results in successful student learning."

In addition to the assessment method used, the assessor must consider the classroom context in which teaching and learning occur, which can be completed by classroom observation. Portfolios, too, are popular tools for teacher evaluation systems, and Florida's assessment system of tasks forms the basis for a portfolio. If portfolios are to be used as part of an assessment system, they should be explicitly linked to the performance-based standards that form the foundation of the assessment system with clearly defined expectations and consistency.

As a result of Florida's requirement that each school district align its assessment system with state standards, the "district assessment systems for alternatively prepared teachers have dramatically improved," according to the authors. Through proper training of assessors and continued vigilance, the authors conclude that "assessment systems are the key to successful alternative educator preparation programs."

They should know. Eileen McDaniel is senior educational program director for communication and policy development, Bureau of Educator Certification, Florida Department of Education, in Tallahassee. One of McDaniel's major contributions to the bureau and to her customers is a monthly newsletter that goes to all of the district certification contacts. For some time, districts had been requesting this communication tool, which now keeps the districts informed of certification changes, issues, and updates and suggests ways that districts can help the bureau perform more efficiently.

Now an education consultant, Karen Wilde was previously the program director of the Florida Department of Education's Bureau of Educator

Certification. Wilde has written widely about the Florida Alternative Certification Program.

In dealing with program implementation, Michael McKibbin shares organizational and goal-setting tips in Chapter 6. Not only does McKibbin present the rationale for development of the alternate route in California, but he includes some of the consequences to the program as a result of legislative changes. For example, with the ebb and flow of teacher needs, alternate route programs have developed or expanded programs to meet the demand. Early on, elementary teachers were most in demand; more recently, the need for more special education teachers has led the demand. In 2005, alternative routes to certification prepared more than half of California's mathematics teachers.

An advantage of alternate route programs is clearly that the program often can adapt quickly to new demands, as McKibbin explains. Frequently, this adaptability keeps programs viable and strong. Another feature that keeps programs strong is candidate recruitment from among special populations such as men, ethnic and racial minority groups, and retiring military personnel in addition to career switchers.

"The best alternative routes to certification (ARC) programs are those that involve the school districts who hire the candidates," writes McKibbin. "Shared power increases the power of all participants." McKibbin recommends that collaboration and power sharing begin early in the program because joint planning—from selection through hiring—can make a difference to the teacher candidate's development. Similarly, a shared instructional program by teachers and faculty provides learning and discussion opportunities that can benefit the ARC candidate.

McKibbin writes, "finding support providers is one of the greatest challenges for ARC programs," adding that not all teachers want to be support providers any more than all teachers should be support providers. McKibbin suggests that in some schools, support providers are "start-up coaches" and may include retired teachers. In his surveys of ARC candidates, McKibbin reports that "a reflective and systematic peer support system (cohort) makes a huge difference in the long-term success" of an alternative route to certification program.

This and other lessons from experience are helpful guidelines toward implementing a successful alternate route program. McKibbin knows those lessons from experience; for 22 years, he has worked for the state of California, currently for the California Commission on Teacher Credentialing. McKibbin has had responsibilities relating to the development and implementation of laws concerning the preparation and certification of teachers, including California's alternative certification programs. Previously he was a faculty member at four universities, associate director of a small education research company, and a teacher at both the elementary and high school levels.

Each of the authors of the chapters in this book has provided general guidelines and some practical and useful ways in which a program administrator can achieve success for candidates in all pathways to teaching programs.

2

Recruitment and Selection

Michelle Rhee and David Keeling
The New Teacher Project

Year after year, two fundamental questions confront school districts across the country: First, how can we attract teacher candidates to apply? And second, how can we identify those applicants who would be good teachers from those who would not? The answers, of course, are recruitment and selection. Together, these two components form the foundation of any effective teacher hiring initiative. Without a recruitment campaign that succeeds in attracting high-quality teacher candidates, the school district cannot create a pool of applicants adequate to meet its quality and quantity goals; without consistent, rigorous selection criteria and assessment tools, the district cannot guarantee that the candidates it chooses are the best available. Increasingly, alternate route to teacher certification programs are playing important roles in school districts' efforts to staff their schools effectively. But what can these programs teach us about bringing applicants to a district's door or identifying which candidates are best suited to teach?

Charged with creating a new stream of teacher candidates from the vast pool of Americans who initially chose different careers, alternate route to certification programs have developed a reputation for innovation in these two areas. They have assembled new recruitment tools and marketing strategies to reach the types of high-achieving career changers they seek and to compete successfully against the practiced human resources (HR) offices of the corporate world. Faced with an applicant pool lacking a background in teaching, they have gradually devised new methods of evaluating each candidate's potential for success in the classroom. From their successes, school systems can draw broader lessons in effective teacher hiring practice.

Over the past 10 years, The New Teacher Project (TNTP) has gained significant experience in the design and development of highly selective alternate routes to certification and built particular expertise in teacher recruitment and selection. A national nonprofit organization founded by former urban school teachers, TNTP's mission is (1) to increase the number of outstanding individuals who become public school teachers and (2) to create environments for all educators that allow them to maximize their impact on student achievement. Working hand in hand with the nation's largest public school systems, TNTP has successfully recruited, prepared, and/or certified approximately 23,000 high-quality teachers since its inception in 1997. Of these new teachers, approximately 16,000 were hired through TNTP's alternate route to teacher certification programs, which currently serve school districts in the cities of Baltimore, Chicago, Miami, New York, Philadelphia, Oakland, and Washington, D.C., among others. In 2006 alone, TNTP's programs attracted a total of almost 30,000 applications and had an average acceptance rate of just 14%, making them comparable in selectivity to such institutions as Harvard, Stanford, or Yale.

TNTP has been able to achieve these results by constantly pursuing innovations and improvements in the way it attracts and selects new teacher candidates. Today, TNTP uses a recruitment model that emphasizes data-driven decision making and a toolbox of strategies that can be customized to the specific needs of the school districts that its programs serve. Then, with the conviction that only the most talented individuals should be privileged to educate our nation's children, TNTP uses a rigorous research-based selection model to evaluate each applicant's core characteristics and abilities objectively and make informed admissions decisions. This chapter discusses TNTP's approach to these critical components of alternate route to certification programs, with a focus on best practices and lessons learned. Although the majority of the strategies discussed were initially developed exclusively for use by alternate route programs, TNTP believes that almost all can be used to improve school districts' overall teacher hiring efforts with minimal modification.

Common Barriers to Recruitment and Selection

Improving teacher recruitment and selection depends on first understanding how the existing system functions and where it tends to break down. TNTP's experience implementing alternate route to teacher certification programs and working side by side with school districts' HR departments has shown that they have in common three major types of challenges, including unfocused recruitment strategies, flawed application and hiring processes, and inconsistent selection practices. Each of these common challenges is described in greater detail here.

Unfocused Recruitment Strategies

Job postings. Newspaper advertisements. Career fairs. These are all common elements of teacher recruitment campaigns, but all too commonly they are the *only* elements. In the competitive marketplace from which alternate route programs must draw their applicants, such strategies are simply insufficient; luring people from stable high-paying careers or competing against the aggressive HR departments of today's businesses takes more than that. Yet many school districts rely on rudimentary marketing tactics and a scattershot approach to attracting candidates. Lacking a clear sense of what types of applicants the district is seeking or how many it actually needs to recruit to produce the desired number of teachers, the district's staff casts as wide a net as possible, catching many applicants they do not want or need while missing others that they do.

Likewise, without a distinctive program identity or a recruitment strategy that integrates and reinforces key messages, they confuse applicants and miss critical opportunities to build awareness of the program. Finally, many fail to recognize the importance of being proactive about finding applicants who are interested and eligible to teach the highest need subjects (math and science, for example), instead relying on an essentially passive approach that treats these candidates no differently than the rest.

Flawed Application and Hiring Processes

In many cases, even when teacher recruitment programs do succeed in getting candidates to take the initial steps toward applying, they lose these candidates because of convoluted and inefficient application and hiring procedures that cause delays and suggest that individual candidates are unimportant. TNTP's 2003 study, *Missed Opportunities: How We Keep High-Quality Teachers Out of Urban Classrooms,* showed that urban school systems lose 30% to 60% of all teacher applicants because of delays in the application and hiring process that leave them in limbo for months. Not only that, but the report showed that the best qualified candidates—the ones with the most job options—were the first to withdraw from the process. Bureaucratic obstacles, inattentive customer service, poor quality control, and ineffective data collection systems further complicate this problem and send a devastating message to prospective candidates, who quickly begin to feel unvalued (Levin & Quinn, 2003).

Inconsistent Selection Processes

For school districts, the importance of choosing the right teacher is obvious; the impact of an unqualified or poorly performing teacher on his or her students can be devastating. For alternate route to certification programs, choosing the right teacher is also important because the quality of the program's participants weighs so heavily on its reputation and ability to be successful in other areas, from building public support for the program to ensuring that school principals want to hire the candidates the program recruits and trains. It seems obvious, then, that creating and refining the processes and tools that a school district uses to evaluate and hire new teachers should be an absolute priority. However, many school districts and alternate route programs lack meaningful selection criteria beyond basic eligibility requirements, provide little formalized training for selectors, and rely on faulty assessment tools. As a result, high-quality candidates cannot be identified accurately or consistently, and the question of whether the individuals who are hired would actually make effective, dedicated teachers is left unresolved.

A Different Approach

It is easy enough to point out these types of challenges and obstacles, and TNTP's experience working with public school systems has shown that many of those engaged in the task of finding and hiring new teachers already recognize these problems but are unsure how to overcome them. If flyers, newspaper advertisements, and career fairs are not enough, what does truly effective recruitment involve? How can a program find more math and science candidates when so often it seems these individuals are nowhere to be found? What types of characteristics are indicative of someone with high teaching potential, and how can those characteristics be evaluated?

Over the last 6 years, TNTP has attempted to find answers to these kinds of questions through its alternate route to certification programs. Faced with the challenge of meeting the needs of its partner school districts in ever more cost-effective, efficient, and high-quality ways, TNTP has accumulated a wealth of institutional knowledge about how best to attract large numbers of applicants to become teachers for hard-to-staff schools and how to determine which of them has the greatest potential for success in the classroom. To illustrate how TNTP approaches new teacher recruitment and selection, let's create a hypothetical alternate route to teacher certification program and walk through the key strategies, activities, and processes TNTP believes are necessary to make it a success. Again, many, if not all, of these strategies and systems can be applied to a school district's hiring efforts more broadly.

Recruiting a Diverse Pool of High-Quality Applicants

For the purposes of this discussion, let's use the city of Detroit as the site of the program. Like many other urban school districts, Detroit faces chronic challenges finding qualified teachers for its schools. Determined to improve student achievement, the school district's leadership decides to start an alternate route to certification program to bring in a new stream of talented teachers, especially those eligible to teach shortage-area subjects. Under pressure to fill classroom vacancies before the coming school year, the new program administrator hurries off to work on what is clearly the first priority: building an applicant pool.

Starting at the Ending: Forecasting Needs, Setting Goals, and Using Data

TNTP begins every teacher recruitment program at its ending—that is, by focusing on the number and type of teachers the program must successfully place in actual classrooms. Say that the Detroit Public School District has charged the program with producing a total of 100 new teachers, of whom at least half must be eligible to teach the high-need subject areas of math, science, and special education. What does it take to get 100 teachers into actual classrooms? How many applications must the program attract? The answers to these questions will shape the entire recruitment strategy.

The purpose of the recruitment campaign is to create a pool of applicants large enough to allow the program to be selective in whom it accepts. At first glance, it seems reasonable to suggest that 300, 400, or 500 applications should be more than enough to yield 100 teachers. However, determining an adequate number of applicants is in fact far more complicated. Some applicants will not meet the program's eligibility requirements. Others will be eliminated through the selection process or simply decide, after submitting their applications, not to pursue the program after all. From the very beginning, extremely few will be eligible to teach high-need subjects. Suddenly, 500 applications begins to seem inadequate.

Today, TNTP relies on average conversion data from its programs nationwide to project how many applicants will be eligible, how many of those applicants will be invited to interview, how many interviewees will be accepted, and so on. In all, TNTP looks at more than a dozen conversion points, assigning a percentage for each based on historical data and key assumptions (e.g., estimating that of all applications received, 90% will include all required components). Breaking down the total number of teachers to be hired through the program in this way immediately gives program staff a reasonably accurate and realistic indication of how many applications are needed (in this case, TNTP would project a need for nearly 800). The program can then begin formulating a recruitment strategy around this number, setting benchmarks for overall application numbers and specific targets for applications from high-need candidates. In addition, the program can monitor projected versus actual conversion rates throughout the application period and make appropriate adjustments to account for any discrepancies.

At this point, TNTP also takes into consideration differences in the projected number of applications needed to yield a high-need teacher from the number required to yield a teacher for lower-need subjects; for example, TNTP has found that, on average, it takes about seven applications to fill one high school math position with a qualified candidate versus only three applications to fill an elementary school position.

This backward-design goal-setting process exemplifies the data-driven nature of TNTP's approach to new teacher recruitment, which characterizes the rest of the program as well. In fact, TNTP relies on data—whether actual, from the program at hand, or projected, based on information from other programs it has developed—as an integral part of its decision-making process. For example, TNTP programs use marketing data to continually evaluate the cost effectiveness of their recruitment strategies. Using information from applicants about how they learned about the program, staff members monitor results daily, determine a specific return on investment (ROI) for every strategy, from Internet advertising to on-campus recruiting, and then reallocate recruitment funding (often within days) to those strategies that demonstrate the greatest success. This helps ensure that the program is using limited resources wisely and maximizing the impact of the campaign overall.

TNTP believes that using data to drive decision making is the only way to ensure that a teacher recruitment initiative is as effective as possible. However, this approach requires that the data in consideration are consistently accurate and reliable. Thus, another major component of TNTP's alternate route to teacher certification programs is the implementation of data tracking and reporting systems that facilitate the collection and analysis of applicant information. More importantly, TNTP trains its staff to be data oriented and establishes processes to support both formal and informal assessments of program progress (e.g., by creating automated reports that any staff member can run from the program's database, allowing for up-to-the-minute information about the applicant pool). Behind all of this is an advanced technological system that can capture, store, and organize data efficiently (for more information, see "Entering the Matrix: Leveraging Technology" later in this chapter).

Learning to Talk: Building a Brand and Creating Compelling Messages

Now that the goal of applicants to be recruited is set (approximately 800) and the program has put its data-tracking systems in place, the next step is to shape the program's image in a way that makes it attractive to prospective candidates. Major corporations have relied on brand recognition as a crucial marketing strategy since the 19th century, when companies making products like Quaker Oats and Campbell's soup began trying to build customer familiarity with their packaging. Since then, these practices have grown ever more complex and sophisticated, as corporations like Disney, Coca-Cola, Intel, and Nike seek to achieve worldwide recognition for their products. With their success in mind, each of TNTP's recruitment programs is built around a unique branding effort that draws public attention to the program and promotes easy recall of key information. Programs receive a unique program name, logo, tagline, and appearance, all of which remain consistent throughout all of their marketing materials and Website.

Let's start with the program name. Including the name of the city targeted by the program clearly makes sense; in addition to specifying the scope of the program, Detroit is among the country's most storied cities, so using its name up front may help draw in candidates from other areas of the country. At the same time, those who already live in Detroit may take pride in joining a program affiliated with their home city.

Along the same lines, it also makes sense to incorporate "teaching" or "teachers" in the program name, again with the goal of giving the public an immediate sense of the program's purpose (TNTP uses its brand of Teaching Fellows names, such as Miami Teaching Fellows, New York City Teaching Fellows, and DC Teaching Fellows for its programs). For the purposes of this exercise, let's assume this is a TNTP-affiliated program and call it the "Detroit Teaching Fellows"; however, other combinations could be equally effective (e.g., "Teach Detroit" or "New Teachers for a New Detroit").

"Detroit Teaching Fellows" begins to convey some basic information about the program, but the name alone is not enough to communicate its core purpose or goals. At the same time, the program needs to be able to summarize this information in a way that is memorable and easy to understand for potential applicants. Defining a short program tagline or motto fulfills this need (e.g., TNTP's Oakland Teaching Fellows program uses this tagline: "Bringing outstanding professionals to the urban classroom"). In creating a tagline, TNTP first attempts to answer questions like these:

- What kinds of people does the program want to attract?
- In what types of schools will new teachers be teaching?
- What is the primary message the program wants to send?
- What community characteristics should the program reflect?
- What makes this program different from others?

Because the program is an alternate route to certification and school district leaders want to tap into Detroit's many professionals, the tagline might emphasize words like *professionals* or *career changers*. This may also help differentiate the program from others that the school district's HR department operates to recruit traditionally certified teachers to its schools. Because Detroit Teaching Fellows will be needed primarily in low-performing schools, it is important to make this clear from the beginning as well, perhaps by employing phrases like "urban schools," "inner-city schools," or "Detroit's most challenged schools." Many school districts are hesitant to use such straightforward language in their recruitment materials, but by confronting these issues head on, the program will send a message that candidates are truly needed and can make a difference in these communities. Finally, the tagline may incorporate region- or city-specific themes, language, or images (e.g., Detroit's moniker "the motor city"). By using language cleverly, the program can make the tagline both communicative and memorable.

Across the board, TNTP programs embrace clear, compelling, and, most of all, *honest* messages. To draw smart, high-performing individuals into the teaching profession, TNTP believes that alternate route to certification programs must appeal to their desire to address social inequities and do something that truly matters. These programs utilize recruitment campaigns that send the message that the children of the city, many of them the poorest children, are not receiving the education they deserve. Whereas many advertisements seeking new teachers rely on the worn and ultimately unconvincing images of smiling kids, perfect red apples, and sunshine-yellow school buses, these campaigns paint a starker, more realistic (and often troubling) picture that serves as a challenge to those who see them. As an early advertisement for TNTP's DC Teaching Fellows program read, "Two out of three of our third graders can't read at grade level. Do something about it. Teach" (see Figure 2.1).

Perhaps not surprisingly, officials at many school districts are skeptical about running this type of ad. They often feel that the "negative" message would not inspire people to join the program. Ultimately, however, the opposite is true; *only* these kinds of messages are capable of compelling people who already have stable high-paying jobs (or the prospect of getting such a job) to work in a public school where they will likely be paid far less, lose many of the comforts of a corporate career, and face a completely new set of day-to-day challenges. These candidates are motivated not by images of smiling children that suggest everything is fine, but by a deeper desire to play a meaningful and positive role in their communities or to right a wrong. Honest, hard-hitting ads like those TNTP creates send a clear message to prospective applicants that the district recognizes the problem, is serious about addressing it, and needs their help. In the end, the thousands of applications that TNTP's campaigns attract year after year are a testament to their effectiveness.

Figure 2.1   DC Teaching Fellows Advertisement

Source: The New Teacher Project.

Of course, along with all the motivating messages must come the more mundane program communications, but these too are critical. Among other things, the program must clearly and repeatedly emphasize its application filing deadlines to ensure prospective candidates act on their burgeoning interest in doing something that matters. Likewise, the program should clearly define the application process from start to finish so candidates know exactly what to expect and when to expect it. Again, the kind of individuals the program is seeking typically have multiple employment options, many of which pay better than teaching. Becoming a teacher is a risk they will not take unless they feel part of a well-organized process that respects their time, experience, and commitment.

Finally, not all applicants are created equal; although the program's tagline and primary messages should appeal to a variety of high-achieving people, other messages may be necessary to attract certain subsets of the applicant pool. For example, TNTP has found that math and science candidates are especially interested in sharing their content-specific knowledge with students. Special education candidates, in contrast, often have had personal experience with a child with special needs. TNTP's programs take this kind of information into account and create specialized messages designed to resonate with the interests and motivations of these candidate groups. A message from one TNTP program oriented toward potential math candidates provides a good example: "Your job is all about numbers. Now it can be about students."

Getting in the Game: Using Aggressive Marketing Strategies

Having established some core messages and a compelling tagline, the Detroit Teaching Fellows is now prepared to begin recruiting candidates. The question now is how to increase the program's visibility to the public and pique the interest of potential applicants.

To attract the most qualified individuals, the program needs to use a variety of recruitment strategies that take the process beyond mere advertising. TNTP relies on such methods as Internet marketing, print advertising, grassroots outreach, and candidate cultivation to reach out to high-achieving individuals and entice them to apply. A variety of coordinated recruitment materials (such as flyers, postcards, newspaper and radio advertisements, and other marketing collateral) support these strategies and encourage interested candidates to visit the program's interactive Website (discussed in greater detail later).

A good starting place is to pinpoint who is responsible for the recruiting effort. TNTP believes that well-trained full-time recruiters are essential to a successful alternate route program. Those charged with recruiting new teacher candidates are often HR staff or other personnel who also have many other responsibilities. In these situations, recruitment too often takes a backseat to other pressing tasks. But TNTP's programs specifically seek out determined individuals to serve as full-time program recruiters and make attracting applicants their central responsibility.

In addition to posting job listings on Internet Websites, distributing flyers, answering candidate questions, and facilitating program information sessions, recruiters make connections with local leaders and career service offices and make presentations on campuses and before community groups. In larger programs, recruiters may be assigned specific types of candidates to target; for example, one recruiter might be charged with attracting applications specifically from math and science candidates, and another might be accountable for special education candidates. By defining each recruiter's role in this way, the program encourages these critical employees to create lasting networks and develop expertise within their area.

In some cases, the full-time recruiters hired by TNTP programs are also backed by a group of current teachers who serve as part-time "teacher ambassadors." These teachers are paid by the program to aid in the recruitment of new teachers to the district. They work several hours per week for a few months during the program's peak application season. Among other activities, they participate in information sessions and make phone calls to candidates. As active teachers, these individuals are uniquely able to speak to the many concerns and questions of applicants, and they are also uniquely able to increase applicants' enthusiasm for a teaching career. Teacher ambassadors are carefully selected based on their personality traits, experience, and fit with the program's philosophy. Prior to beginning their recruitment duties, ambassadors take part in 5 to 7 hours of training in the elements of the program, how best to communicate with potential applicants, what strategies to use, and how to help meet the target recruitment goals and timelines.

Given the program's target of 100 teachers, let's say the Detroit Teaching Fellows decides to hire one full-time recruiter and six teacher ambassadors. The program can now focus on making itself known to the public. Specifically, the program needs to create effective materials to support the

---

Building a Buzz

In all of its projects, TNTP coordinates a wide array of recruitment tactics to maximize the effectiveness of the campaign and to generate a buzz around the target area. For instance, an advertising campaign will be launched on the radio and in local newspapers; simultaneously, TNTP begins a mass e-mail campaign to community leaders and previously identified candidate sources. Messages in each publicize the program in general and alert recipients to upcoming 60-minute information sessions in the area, which serve the dual purpose of providing details about the program and inspiring attendees to apply. Meanwhile, TNTP recruiters conduct an aggressive outreach effort on local college campuses and post flyers and posters in heavily trafficked areas of the city. This type of coordinated communications strategy ensures that the program gains maximum visibility among its target populations quickly and attracts the largest number of applicants possible.

marketing effort and identify a number of channels through which to expose prospective applicants to these materials. TNTP's experience has shown that developing a universal design scheme (one that can be adapted easily into a flyer, postcard, business card, or print advertisement) is one of the most cost-effective and flexible approaches to the design and production of materials. To increase brand recognition, it is important to coordinate colors, images, and overall tone across all materials and the program Website. In general, the materials produced by the program should have these characteristics:

- Vivid, compelling, and professional in appearance
- Action oriented, directing interested candidates to the Website for additional information or providing clear instructions for applying
- Adaptable to a variety of formats, sizes, and media
- Easy to produce and distribute in terms of size, layout, and material type

Figure 2.2 shows an example of the type and quality of materials TNTP's programs produce.

Figure 2.2   Sample Program Flyer / Advertisement

Source: The New Teacher Project.

Armed with training and materials like these, the Detroit Teaching Fellows' recruitment staff can start drawing in large numbers of applicants. However, recruitment does not stop there; although getting candidates in the door is obviously important, ensuring that they complete the application process and enroll in the program (if accepted) are also among the recruiter's responsibilities. This is particularly important with regard to applicants who are eligible to teach high-need subject areas. With so few of these individuals available, the program must dedicate special attention to maximizing the number of candidates who actually become teachers.

This is where candidate cultivation enters the picture. The main goal of cultivation is to establish regular personal connections between a potential teacher and the program to convert these candidates from one stage of the process to another (e.g., so candidates who begin their application complete it, so candidates who receive an offer accept it, and so on). This contact can take many forms, including mailings, e-mails, e-mailed newsletters, phone calls, and events. In a way, cultivation is customer service taken to the extreme, anticipating candidates' interests and needs and shepherding them through the application and hiring process. Candidate cultivation does not necessarily require an enormous budget or a complicated strategy; in fact, the best cultivation strategies are based simply on thoughtful and timely interactions with candidates that emphasize their importance as individuals and make them feel valued. The tactics that cultivation involves can seem obvious, but they take time and energy to implement systematically, which ultimately is what makes them effective.

TNTP's Oakland Teaching Fellows program offers a good example of creative candidate cultivation at work. The program has implemented a comprehensive tactical effort to reach out to potential applicants who meet minimum eligibility requirements to teach mathematics. Through the initiative, program staff members search through application files to locate those applicants who qualify, then send e-mails to those candidates asking whether they have considered teaching math, one of the highest-need subjects in education today. Prospective applicants receive an invitation to attend a special recruiting event that generates excitement about the program and creates a sense of connectivity among the potential new teachers. The program follows up with personalized phone calls from recruiters and teacher ambassadors to answer candidates' questions and continue emphasizing their importance to Oakland's schools and students. Again, the underlying strategies involved in this effort are relatively simple—targeted e-mails, phone calls, face-to-face communication, and follow-up—but for applicants who may be uncertain, these personal touches and extra attention may become the deciding factors in whether they later join the program.

Entering the Matrix: Leveraging Technology to Improve Results

Many of the high-achieving candidates that alternate route to teacher certification programs seek out come from the private sector or directly from colleges or universities. These applicants are generally accustomed to using computers and other technological tools every day. In particular, the newest college graduates—for whom online shopping is old news, blogging is routine, and high-speed Internet is practically a necessity—are extremely comfortable managing their lives online and have come to expect the type of anywhere, anytime access to information that the Internet offers. Moreover, as computers have grown more powerful and Websites and databases easier to create, technological systems are increasingly important to promoting program efficiency and cost effectiveness.

For these reasons, the Detroit Teaching Fellows program will rely heavily on technology—from interactive tools for applicants to Web-based data management systems—to support core program processes and maximize results. To begin with, an interactive high-quality Website functions as the centerpiece of the recruitment campaign. Flyers, postcards, advertisements, and job postings promote the Website heavily in an effort to drive candidates to learn more about the program and apply. Created by professional designers and updated regularly by program staff, the Website maintains a professional appearance consistent with other program materials and is characterized by a direct and easy-to-use format. By offering extensive program information and a variety of Web-based tools to applicants and accepted candidates, the Website plays a key role in program operations and communications. Easy to update and instantly available to anyone with Internet access, it provides the program with a highly efficient way to disseminate information and keep applicants abreast of any changes.

Importantly, the program Website is integrated with TNTP's TeacherTrack applicant tracking software, which improves the ability of program staff to monitor key data, conduct quality control checks, and communicate with candidates. TNTP developed TeacherTrack based on its familiarity with school hiring practices and extensive experience with implementing and managing teacher recruitment and hiring campaigns for major school districts across the country. Among other things, TeacherTrack enables the program to:

- Accept, store, and organize online applications, including résumés and cover letters.
- Generate automated communications to candidates.

- Prescreen applicants for initial quality assessments and program eligibility online.
- Record candidate eligibility for specific subject areas.
- Offer online interview event scheduling (and automatic event reminders) to applicants.
- Record the results of candidate interviews.
- Notify candidates of their status in the application process.
- Monitor candidate conversion rates.
- Offer principals the ability to review the application materials of accepted applicants.
- Track the placement of program participants.
- Generate predefined reports and queries regarding the recruitment, selection and hiring process (e.g., number of applicants, number of hires, etc.).

By streamlining the recruitment, selection, and placement process, TeacherTrack enables program staff to focus on providing exceptional customer service as well as selecting the highest quality candidates, rather than tracking paperwork. TeacherTrack also allows program staff to communicate easily with and prioritize specific groups in the applicant pool, such as those applicants eligible to teach shortage subject areas.

But suppose the Detroit Teaching Fellows is operating on a budget that makes investing in a system like TeacherTrack unfeasible. That does not mean effective data tracking is out of the question. Even simple, relatively basic systems, like those that can be created through software such as Microsoft Access, can be invaluable to the program if carefully maintained and updated.

The Devil in the Details: Creating a Customer Service–Oriented Culture

As applications begin to flow in, the staff of the Detroit Teaching Fellows quickly becomes immersed in the day-to-day concerns of processing applications, responding to e-mail and phone messages, sending out mailings, and carrying out the strategies of the program's recruitment plan. The pace only increases as the application season rolls onward and deadlines approach. In this environment, it is easy to let things slide: A phone call goes unanswered. An applicant's file gets misplaced. Candidates with questions get passed from person to person, receiving different answers from each.

The program's goal must be to ensure that these seemingly minor mistakes and problems occur as infrequently as possible. Although the program may be dealing with hundreds of applicants, each individual applicant has relatively little contact with the program; if even one of those experiences is a negative one (e.g., the applicant receives incorrect information or is treated poorly), it colors that individual's perception of the entire program. Not only that, but it may affect others' perceptions of the program as well because the applicant tells all her friends about her disappointing interaction with a program representative.

With the recognition that details matter, TNTP endeavors to instill a customer-service mentality among all program staff. TNTP's approach in this respect is centered on the core conviction that teachers are professionals who deserve respect and appreciation, and that those who are contemplating a teaching career should be similarly valued and encouraged. Customer service for TNTP means not only the usual things, like being positive, courteous, and responsive in all interactions with candidates, but also respecting each candidate's time, trust, and commitment.

As a result, TNTP programs aspire to operate in a highly organized and professional manner, to minimize turnaround times (for example, in 2005, the average length of time between receipt of an application and completion of the initial screening process in New York was just 1.5 days), and to build in tight quality control mechanisms to ensure that, for instance, a letter is not sent to the wrong person or a candidate's application materials are lost. In the rare instances where a mistake does occur, the program staffers acknowledge it, apologize, and do whatever it takes to rectify the situation.

TNTP's alternate route to certification programs also empower all staff members—regardless of their actual job responsibilities—to answer basic questions about the program and resolve problems as necessary. If the staff member lacks the right information, it is his or her responsibility to guide the candidate personally to someone who can help. The goal, in this case, is to get applicants the information they need as quickly as possible without providing inaccurate information. Program staff are also trained to reinforce key messages during any interaction with an applicant (e.g., "While I'm accessing your application information, have you registered for your required tests yet?").

Ultimately, a candidate's impression of the alternate route program (and often the school district itself) is created by the gradual accumulation of his or her interactions and experiences with it. The types of strategies just discussed help programs hold on to as many applicants as possible from application to enrollment in the program and hiring by a school. Here it is worth emphasizing again that the most sought-after candidates are typically also the ones with the most options: They will not tolerate rudeness, a pattern of mistakes, or unexplained delays. But if they feel valued and treated fairly, they are much more likely to become Detroit Teaching Fellows.

Recruitment Campaign Checklist

○ Establish overall recruitment goal (i.e., number of teachers to be hired through program).
○ Create specific recruitment targets (e.g., total number of applications, number of applications from math-eligible candidates, etc.).
○ Set up a data collection system to gather and store information on applicants.
○ Track conversion rates (e.g., percentage of applicants who submit a complete application and then are invited to interview).
○ Build a distinct program brand (name, tagline, key messages).
○ Create compelling, adaptable recruitment materials.
○ Hire and train full-time recruiters.
○ Set and publicize clear application deadlines.
○ Implement multiple recruitment strategies and track their cost effectiveness in terms of cost per applicant.
○ Aggressively target and cultivate applicants in high-need subject areas.
○ Train staff in high-quality customer service.

Selecting Top-Quality Candidates

The recruitment team for the Detroit Teaching Fellows has done its job. The program has been profiled by the local media, its advertisements have run in newspapers and on the radio, community groups have embraced it as a strategy to improve area schools, and hundreds of applications have come in from a diverse range of candidates. Amid the ringing phones and stacks of file folders, the program administrator discovers a new challenge has emerged: determining which of the many applicants would actually make a good teacher and which would not.

Over the last two decades, it has become clear that high-quality teachers are the key to increasing student achievement. Studies have shown teacher quality to be the single most important school-based factor influencing student achievement, surpassing school quality and other factors (Hanushek, Kain, & Rivkin, 1998). Other research has shown that the difference between having a good teacher and a bad teacher can be greater than one grade-level equivalent in annual achievement growth for students (Hanushek, 1992), and that the gap in achievement between students taught by less effective teachers and those taught by better teachers can grow as large as 50 percentile points in as few as 3 years (Sanders & Rivers, 1996).

At the same time that the importance of high-quality teachers has become apparent, it has also become clear that urban and high-poverty schools, which struggle in the face of low student achievement, high dropout and absenteeism rates, and disproportionately high percentages of special needs students, are far less likely to have them. In fact, although a teacher's mastery of his or her content area is one of the few clear predictors of teacher quality and, ultimately, student achievement (Monk, 1994), researchers have shown that students in high-poverty schools are 77% more likely to be assigned a teacher who lacks the minimal academic requirements for the subject being taught (Jerrold & Ingersoll, 2002). Other studies have shown that the percentage of teachers teaching under certification waivers and "emergency" credentials is 61% higher in high-poverty schools ("Meeting the Highly Qualified Teacher Challenge," 2003).

To ensure the program is addressing these issues by bringing in only the best qualified individuals among the applicant pool, the Detroit Teaching Fellows needs a way to compare candidates systematically to one another and identify those who are likely to succeed in the classroom. Creating a selection model to accomplish this important task requires the following:

- Establishing a set of clearly delineated selection criteria against which to assess all candidates
- Creating and implementing assessment tools that enable the program to evaluate and document evidence of each candidate's qualities and skills consistently and objectively
- Implementing an application screening process that quickly eliminates clearly unsuitable candidates from the selection process and identifies those with potential
- Designing an activity-based interview process that seeks to gain detailed information about candidates by observing how they respond in real time to realistic situations and challenges
- Training selectors to use the selection criteria and tools effectively and fairly, and to represent the program in a professional manner
- Setting up a quality control and review process, to ensure that the decisions the program makes are consistent and fair and do not allow unfit candidates to become teachers.

What Makes a Good Teacher?: Defining Effective Selection Criteria

Clear, appropriate, and specific selection criteria are essential to any high-quality alternate route to certification program. These criteria form the basis for the program's decisions about the quality of each candidate. The most basic criteria spell out the program's requirements as they relate to the passage of state-required exams, the candidate's undergraduate grade-point average (GPA), prior experience, and so on. The best selection criteria, however, go much deeper, defining the qualities that characterize truly effective teachers.

Figure 2.3   Three-Stage Selection Process

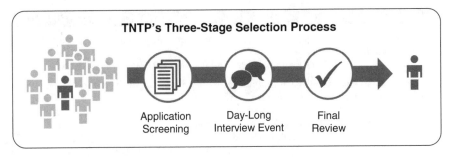

In recognition of the crucial role teacher quality plays in student learning, TNTP takes the task of candidate selection very seriously. Through 9 years of research and experience identifying high-quality teachers, TNTP has found that an important determinant of a teacher's future success in the classroom is the nature of his or her fundamental personality and character traits. Therefore, TNTP programs employ a specific manageable list of selection criteria that identify and define as comprehensively as possible the characteristics and traits that the most successful teachers have, regardless of their prior experience or training in education. In particular, TNTP looks for evidence of these qualities:

- Critical thinking
- Prior achievement
- Personal responsibility
- Commitment to raising academic achievement
- Constant learning from past experiences
- Sensitivity to and respect for differing norms of interaction
- Effective communication skills

TNTP's selection model aims to gain a holistic view of each candidate's qualities through a three-stage evaluation process. Figure 2.3 illustrates the basic components of this process.

Measuring Up: Assembling Effective Assessment Tools and Rubrics

The quality of the tools used to evaluate prospective teachers can make or break an alternate route to teacher certification program. If not carefully constructed, the program's evaluation tools inevitably fail to gauge candidates' strengths and weaknesses effectively or consistently, thereby threatening the validity of the entire process. At the core of TNTP's selection model is a comprehensive rubric that defines the selection criteria, provides

Figure 2.4   Selection Rubric

Elements of a Rubric	Selection Model
Criteria serve as the basis for judgment.	This model is built on seven criteria called "competencies." Example of one competency: **CRITICAL THINKING**
Definitions and **examples** clarify the meaning of criteria.	Each competency is "defined" along with examples called "indicators." Example of one competency's definition: **Critical Thinking:** • Analyzes situations thoroughly and generates effective strategies. • Discerns the presence and nature of problems accurately. • Develops creative solutions. • Displays logical approach to all situations. **Examples of Critical Thinking Indicators as seen in the Teaching Sample:** • Has a clearly stated goal. • Has a logical beginning, middle, end. • Events or activities show logical progression toward goal. • Material and concepts are reasonable for the age group. • Reasonable amount of information presented for 5 minutes. • Materials or subjects are engaging.
A **scale of values** rates criteria.	Competencies are rated as **(E)** exemplary, **(FA)** fully acceptable, and **(NFA)** not fully acceptable.

indicators for each criterion (i.e., examples of behaviors, skills, or knowledge that indicate the applicant's ability/proficiency in that area), establishes a scale of values by which to rate applicants against the criteria, and provides a place for selectors to make notes and document each candidate's performance during the assessment. Figure 2.4 illustrates the key components of this type of rubric.

Once the interview process begins, program selectors use the rubric to guide them in candidate evaluation, looking for specific behaviors and skills (indicators) that the program has linked to certain criteria. For example, in Figure 2.4, the selector would attempt to assess the applicant's critical thinking skills by watching him teach a sample lesson. During the lesson, the selector makes notes about the candidate's performance: Did he state the goal of the lesson clearly? How did he respond to problems? Was he articulate and engaging? The information the selector gains forms the basis for rating the candidate's ability in this area. The rubric provides space for the selector to repeat this type of analysis for each selection criterion across the various components of the interview event (described in greater detail later in this section).

Reading Between the Lines: Getting the Most Out of Candidates' Application Materials

Before the Detroit Teaching Fellows can begin interviewing, the program first needs a quick way to eliminate candidates who do not meet its eligibility requirements or who are clearly unsuitable to become teachers; spending the time to interview all 800-plus applicants would be impractical and inefficient. The initial application screening (or prescreening) process plays this gatekeeper role. During this time, the Detroit Teaching Fellows uses its own staff and a group of part-time prescreeners to review all candidates' written application materials, including résumés, personal statements in which the applicants respond to a scenario or question posed by the program, academic transcripts, and descriptions of their accomplishments and activities. Through a formal training process, the prescreeners learn how to analyze these materials to confirm that applicants meet eligibility requirements and to identify key indicators of an applicant's potential success.

The goal of the prescreening process is not to come up with a definitive answer as to whether the candidate would be a good teacher but instead to assess the candidate's *potential*. Accordingly, prescreeners only evaluate candidates' abilities in two or three key areas, again using the selection rubric (or an abbreviated version of it) as a guide. Applicants whose written materials show substantial evidence of the selection criteria are "screened in"; the others are "screened out."

The prescreening process immediately weeds out many candidates and provides the Detroit Teaching Fellows with some initial indications as to the remaining applicants' potential effectiveness as teachers. But this first evaluation does not provide the program with enough information to make sound decisions about which candidates should be admitted. To make final decisions, the program first needs to interact with the screened-in candidates face to face and more carefully assess their fundamental qualities and characteristics.

Face Time and Follow-Up: Maximizing the Interview

Interviewing is a standard part of the competitive hiring processes of almost every industry. However, too often interviews are pro forma events characterized by a predictable exchange of vague questions and rehearsed answers that ultimately yield little additional information or benefit to either party. When choosing who will be responsible for the education of our children, this type of perfunctory interview is simply unacceptable.

TNTP takes the concept of the interview to another level, reshaping it as an intensive day-long event (the "Interview Day") that involves multiple components. On Interview Day, trained program interviewers ("selectors") evaluate candidates by looking for further evidence that indicates the extent to which they meet the program's selection criteria. During the course of the

Interview Day, candidates have an opportunity to demonstrate their strengths through several activities, including the following:

- *Teaching a sample lesson:* All candidates are asked to come to Interview Day prepared to teach a small group of their fellow applicants a 5-minute sample lesson. This provides selectors with insight into candidates' ability to create a logical and organized lesson, to present their ideas clearly to a group, and to overcome unexpected challenges.

- *Writing a response to a specific classroom-oriented scenario:* This provides selectors with a window into each candidate's motivations and ability to think and communicate clearly. It also provides an opportunity to see how candidates perform when forced to improvise a response to a challenging situation under the pressure of time constraints.

- *Discussing a typical high-need school scenario with other candidates:* This gives selectors a chance to discern subtle personality traits in applicants by watching their interactions with one another and listening to the kinds of comments they make. Even basic observations—such as who participates least, who tries to negotiate differences in opinion, or who emerges as a leader in the discussion—can be telling.

- *Engaging in a one-on-one interview with a selector:* During the more conventional interview phase of Interview Day, selectors have an opportunity to probe candidates' strengths and weaknesses and to ask questions based on their observations of the candidate during the other parts of the event.

Asking the Right Questions

To assist selectors in making the most thorough and nuanced evaluations of candidates possible, TNTP supplies sample questions that are carefully designed to probe the candidate's skills or abilities with respect to specific selection criteria. These questions are often open ended and require the applicant to discuss his or her response to a real-world situation. Questions to assess an applicant's sense of personal responsibility, for instance, might include ones like these:

- "You have been teaching for 3 months and feel that your students are no better off than they were when you first arrived. What would you do?"
- "Tell me about a time when you were incredibly busy and had to manage multiple responsibilities. How did you handle the situation?"
- "What was the toughest call you had to make in your career or life experience? How did you handle it? What would you do differently if you had the chance?"

TNTP has found that these types of questions are more effective in eliciting meaningful information from applicants about their experience and perspective than those that applicants can easily anticipate and prepare responses to in advance.

Throughout Interview Day, selectors strive to determine whether a candidate should be accepted by:

- Revisiting the résumé and cover letter for evidence of all competencies.
- Evaluating each candidate's performance in all Interview Day components for evidence of the competencies.
- Making a recommendation for acceptance or rejection based on formal ratings captured in the selection rubric supplied by the program.

At the end of Interview Day, selectors review the evidence they have gathered about each candidate in relation to the program's selection criteria. Using the selection rubric, they make a final rating of each candidate's strengths and weaknesses. Based on the candidate's rating in each competency area and their holistic impression of the individual, the selectors note their recommendation and append their evaluation forms and notes.

If Interview Day has gone as planned, candidates leave feeling newly inspired by the program (especially after seeing firsthand the high quality of their fellow applicants) and impressed by its professionalism and organization. Surveys conducted by TNTP in 2005 for its programs nationwide show the extent to which this was the case: on average, 99% of interview candidates said Interview Day increased their desire to join the program; 99% said they were impressed by the other candidates; and 100% said that, overall, Interview Day was a positive experience.

Quality Control: Ensuring the Integrity of the Selection Model

With a solid selection rubric, properly trained selectors, and effective screening and interviewing strategies, the Detroit Teaching Fellows can be

---

Training Selectors

TNTP programs recruit selectors from the schools and districts they serve, including HR staff, assistant principals, principals, and teachers, among others. TNTP ensures the quality of its selectors through a series of intense trainings and workshops held prior to and throughout the application season. New selectors complete a minimum of 8 hours of training that introduces them to the concepts and components that make up TNTP's selection model.

During the training, selectors learn how to use the rubric to recognize evidence of the selection criteria in each component of the interview—the sample teaching lesson, written response, discussion group, and personal interview—by observing and evaluating videotapes of two to three actual candidates. The final training concludes with a 2-hour assessment, which serves as a final exam, as it were, on the selection model.

reasonably sure it is making smart selection decisions and accepting only top-quality candidates. But, mistakes happen. Despite their training, selectors can have unrecognized biases or use the rubric incorrectly. Over time, their sense of what distinguishes a strong candidate from an average candidate may change. Program staff can make data-entry errors. Unless the program devises methods to identify and correct for these kinds of errors, the selection model will gradually shift in significant ways and become compromised.

TNTP programs address these issues by putting in place a series of routine quality control checks and conducting regular retraining of selectors. For example, TNTP requires that selectors carefully document the rationale for their ratings and decisions so this information can be reviewed and confirmed. During a final file review process, the program administrator and other senior staff reexamine each selector's acceptance or rejection recommendations to verify that the candidate in consideration merits the recommendation and meets (or doesn't meet) the program's criteria.

Information about selector decisions that is gathered during the file review process is used by the program to identify any larger problems (e.g., a selector who routinely rates applicants too harshly or leniently in a particular area). Program staff can then address these problems during periodic small- and large-group trainings that respond to trends and issues that arise over the course of the selection season, with the goal of continually improving the selection model's efficacy in identifying the best possible candidates. The selection process includes built-in feedback mechanisms that permit program staff and selectors to identify and rectify problems quickly, regular trainings to norm the criteria selectors use in their decisions, and as-needed corrective trainings to remedy any problems that arise.

Selection Process Checklist

- ○ Define clear selection criteria.
- ○ Establish indicators for each criterion.
- ○ Create a core rubric or other tool with which to evaluate all candidates.
- ○ Use a formal objective rating system to facilitate comparisons of candidates.
- ○ Employ a screening process to identify which candidates should be interviewed.
- ○ Train program selectors through a formal process.
- ○ Maximize the interview through the use of real-life scenarios and activities.
- ○ Review all admissions recommendations.
- ○ Provide regular retraining and/or norming for selectors.

Why Bother?

Like all recruitment and selection strategies, those discussed in this chapter require time, money, and the right people to implement properly. They also demand careful thinking, data tracking, and systematic evaluation. Given all the other challenges and resource limitations facing the Detroit Teaching Fellows program (or, for that matter, any school district), are they really worth it?

TNTP's experience suggests the answer is an unqualified "yes." First, it is again worth emphasizing just how critical recruitment and selection are to any program seeking to fill classrooms with more than just warm bodies. Ineffective recruitment results in a small or uniform applicant pool that prohibits the hiring initiative from being selective. Conversely, even an initiative that attracts thousands of applications can go nowhere without a selection process capable of identifying the best candidates systematically. Either way, the result of poorly planned and executed recruitment and selection strategies is lower quality teachers.

Second, these strategies work. Over the past 6 years, TNTP's alternate routes to certification have challenged the claim that no one wants to teach in urban and high-poverty schools by building extremely large applicant pools and hiring some of the nation's most accomplished citizens to become teachers. In 2005 alone, TNTP's alternate route programs attracted almost 20,000 applications and hired approximately 2,500 high-quality teachers. These new teachers have exceptional academic backgrounds (with degrees from some of the country's most prestigious universities and an average undergraduate GPA of 3.35) and reflect the diversity many school systems are seeking (with 39%, on average, being people of color).

More importantly, these individuals are capable of teaching acute shortage-area subjects like math, science, and special education. In fact, 67% of all new teachers recruited and hired by TNTP programs in 2005 were eligible to teach in a high-need subject area. In some areas of the country, TNTP's alternate route to certification programs are now providing a critical mass of teachers in these subject areas. For example, in New York City, where TNTP has piloted many of the strategies described in this chapter, nearly a quarter (23%) of all active math teachers were originally hired through TNTP's NYC Teaching Fellows program. Of the more than 7,000 Teaching Fellows currently teaching in New York, approximately 55% are assigned to high-need subject area classrooms in general. Today, the program brings in about half of the school system's annual new hires in math, science, and special education.

Not only that, but the teachers that TNTP's programs recruit, select, and train are viewed positively by the school principals with whom they work. On average, 92% of principals surveyed nationwide say they would hire a Teaching Fellow again, and 93% say they are satisfied with the Teaching Fellows in their schools. These high satisfaction ratings point to the efficacy of the selection model these programs utilize and the ability of their recruitment campaigns to draw in high-caliber candidates.

Recent studies of Teaching Fellows' impact on student achievement provide further evidence of their quality as teachers. Two value-added studies conducted of TNTP's New York City Teaching Fellows program (Boyd, Grossman, Lankford, Loeb, & Wycoff, 2005; Kane, Rockoff, & Staiger, 2006) found that:

- By their second and third years in the classroom, Teaching Fellows perform as well as or better than traditionally certified teachers in terms of their effectiveness on student academic outcomes.
- Retention of Fellows is about the same as or even better than that of traditionally certified teachers, despite the fact that Fellows are much more likely to work in high-poverty, high-minority schools with disproportionately low rates of academic success and disproportionately high rates of absenteeism.
- Fellows have more competitive academic backgrounds and score higher on state certification tests than traditionally certified teachers—an important point because research has found a robust link between academic indicators and the influence of teachers on their students' achievement levels (Ferguson, 1991; Ferguson & Ladd, 1996).

Parting Advice for the Detroit Teaching Fellows

"Detroit's students are not getting the education they deserve. We are all responsible for solving this problem." This is the kind of message that the Detroit Teaching Fellows program must live by, as its own challenge and a rallying cry for applicants. Everything the program does must align with this conviction and its underlying commitment to providing Detroit schools with high-quality teachers.

By infusing this sentiment in the program's recruitment materials, its operational processes, and its selection model, the program will maintain a relentless focus on finding the highest quality candidates, treating them professionally, and securing them for Detroit schools. For applicants, it provides the motivation to turn aside other employment options in favor of something meaningful and rewarding, a chance to do something that will have a real impact.

School districts seeking to improve their teacher hiring capacity more generally can benefit from this mission-driven approach as well because this conviction serves as a reminder that reliable data, compelling messages, customer service, and accurate selection tools matter not for their own sake, but because of how much rides on their collective contribution to the program's overall success: the quality of the teachers it produces and the futures of the students who sit in their classrooms.

Working with The New Teacher Project

TNTP offers services like those described in this chapter to public school districts, states, and charter school networks on a contractual basis. Among others, these services include the comprehensive development and management of high-quality alternate routes to teacher certification programs; strategic consulting on teacher hiring and school staffing policies and systems, and new teacher preparation and development. For more information on TNTP's results and services, visit www.tntp.org or e-mail info@tntp.org.

References

Boyd, D., Grossman, P., Lankford, H., Loeb, S., & Wyckoff, J. (2005). *How reduced barriers to entry into teaching changes the teacher workforce and affects student achievement* (NBER Working Paper No. 11844). National Bureau of Economic Research.

Ferguson, R. F. (1991). Paying for public education: New evidence on how and why money matters. *Harvard Journal on Legislation, 28*(2), 465–498.

Ferguson, R. F., & Ladd, H. F. (1996). How and why money matters: An analysis of Alabama schools. In H. F. Ladd (Ed.), *Holding schools accountable*. Washington, DC: Brookings.

Hanushek, E. A. (1992). The trade-off between teacher quantity and quality. *Journal of Political Economy, 100*(1), 84–117.

Hanushek, E. A., Kain, J. F., & Rivkin, S. G. (1998). *Teachers, schools and academic achievement* (NBER Working Paper No. 6691). Cambridge, MA: National Bureau of Economic Research.

Jerald, C. D., & Ingersoll, R. M. (2002). *All talk, no action: Putting an end to out-of-field teaching*. Washington, DC: The Education Trust.

Kane, T., Rockoff, J., & Staiger, D. (2006). What does certification tell us about teacher effectiveness? Evidence from New York City. Unpublished manuscript.

Levin, J., & Quinn, M. (2003). *Missed opportunities: How we keep high-quality teachers out of urban classrooms*. New York: The New Teacher Project.

Meeting the highly qualified teacher challenge: The secretary's second annual report on teacher quality. (2003). Washington, DC: U.S. Department of Education, Office of Policy Planning and Innovation.

Monk, D. H. (1994). Subject area preparation of secondary mathematics and science teachers and student achievement. *Economics of Education Review, 13*(2), 125–145.

Sanders, W. L., & Rivers, J. C. (1996). *Cumulative and residual effects of teachers on future student academic achievement*. Knoxville: University of Tennessee Value-Added Research and Assessment Center.

3

Quality Induction: Mentoring and Support

Ellen Moir

New Teacher Center at the University of California, Santa Cruz

*T*his chapter reviews the background and rationale for the importance of induction and its effectiveness in any alternate route to certification program, explores the key components of a successful induction program, and then defines the issues that must be addressed as a school district begins to delineate its own unique approach to induction.

Historically, new teachers were assigned someone who might be available to give advice. By contrast, an induction program that provides mentors for new teachers, to coach and support them as they begin to put their training into practice, helps bridge the transition from preservice to inservice. Furthermore, it improves teacher quality, fosters student achievement, and contributes to both recruitment and retention of teachers. An effective induction program includes professional development for both the novice teacher and the mentor, training that will make reflection and assessment an ongoing component of the teacher's professional practice.

An executive summary of a study prepared by the National Commission on Teaching and America's Future (Fulton, Yoon, & Lee, 2005) concludes the following:

- Induction should be a stage in a continuum of teacher development.
- Induction should support entry into a learning community.
- Mentoring is a useful component of induction, but only one element of a comprehensive system.
- External networks supported by online technologies can add value.
- Induction is a good investment. (p. 1)

Background and Rationale for Induction

The Impact of an Effective Mentor

Student teaching and traditional or alternate preservice training are necessary steps in creating competent and qualified teaching professionals, but these experiences do not suffice. The impact of being alone in a classroom for the first time can be overwhelming. Providing an exemplary veteran teacher as a mentor, to guide and support the new teacher, can make all the difference in that teacher's success and effectiveness.

Mentors have an impact in ways that no training can match. Effective mentoring supports new teachers in their classrooms, based on the realities they face. The mentor can provide options for solving student and curriculum challenges and make more effective strategic decisions about lesson plans, teaching strategies, and assessment. With this kind of intensive instructional support from the start, new teachers focus less on day-to-day survival and more on ensuring that every student progresses (Achinstein & Athanases, 2006). They become more confident, more skilled, and much more likely to survive their early years in the profession (Smith & Ingersoll, 2004). Their students also benefit, receiving the education they need and deserve.

It is easy to forget what it was like to be a beginning teacher, having to acquire curriculum knowledge and classroom strategies while at the same time balancing practical concerns with lofty ideals. Approaching the problem of teacher retention, it is essential to ask one question: *If I were starting my career today, what would most help me develop into an outstanding, caring, and accomplished teacher?*

One answer stands out among all the rest: "I can only imagine how much better a teacher I would have been that first year if I'd had a mentor. The classroom presents challenges that only those with experience can resolve." Mentors help provide those answers.

Mentors provide practical, concrete advice, model effective teaching techniques in the classroom, and observe the novice teacher nonjudgmentally and then offer feedback in a way that encourages the new teacher to address any concerns. By posing questions to prompt reflection, mentors assist new teachers and can offer another perspective. Their experience helps the novice teacher meld insights from training and professional development with the day-to-day demands of the classroom. The mentor can also act as an advocate for the new teacher in circumstances where the novice cannot act for himself or herself.

Mentors help decrease the isolation of the new teacher. Their emotional support is essential when the obstacles seem insurmountable, and allows the novice to take risks and grow while still keeping the classroom functioning. By developing an individual plan for each new teacher and setting standard-based performance goals to improve teaching practice, mentors create an environment based on collaboration, exchange of ideas, and professionalism. This can then foster a supportive community of educators, which allows mentors to help keep alive the enthusiasm and sense of mission that brought them into the profession and can also enhance the practice of others in the school.

A successful mentoring program can change the face of that first year of teaching ("No Dream Denied," 2003). A new teacher at the end of her first year said, "My adviser kind of walked me through the year. She was always there to listen to my ideas, my reflections. I never felt that I was alone, even when she wasn't in the room, because I knew that I had daily access to a person who would listen and respond to my ideas. I trusted her to give me honest feedback on how successfully a strategy worked . . . she met whatever needs I had."

An Early Example of Mentoring

The California Context   In the mid-1980s, California faced a crisis, one caused primarily by exceptionally low rates of teacher retention. The problems that would eventually visit the rest of the country came early to California, where the student population was increasing in size as well as becoming more diverse. At the same time, the state and many districts were adopting far more complex curricula. Finding and, more importantly, retaining qualified teachers had become almost impossible for many rural and urban districts.

The new teachers who entered this challenging situation were thrown into the classroom with little support beyond their preservice training. Turnover rates were high, particularly among minority teachers. Although a paucity of research on teacher induction had been published at the time, it was obvious that the sink-or-swim method had failed.

As the need to improve the system became clear and state funding became available, the creation of a new program for teacher induction was undertaken, piloted, and ultimately implemented. The design process brought together the entire community of educators: district administrators, principals, union representatives, experienced teachers, new teachers, and Education Department faculty from the University of California, Santa Cruz (UCSC). Together, in 1988, this group designed a comprehensive new teacher support program, with mentoring at its core. One of the pilot programs developed into the Santa Cruz New Teacher Project (SCNTP), led by UCSC in partnership with the Santa Cruz County Office of Education and all the school districts in the area. It began its work with 42 exemplary elementary teachers who were released full time, acted as mentors, and provided individualized support.

The Santa Cruz New Teacher Project   After the first three years, funding lapsed, but the success of the statewide effort and the impact of the induction programs served as models for statewide reform. In 1992, California policymakers enacted SB 1422, which implemented Beginning Teacher Support and Assessment (BTSA) legislation, providing funding for mentor-based programs throughout the state. These BTSA programs ultimately constituted a redesign of the state's credentialing requirements. The final stages in teacher credentialing, which were previously administered by institutions of higher learning, are now integrated into a comprehensive induction system with mentoring at its core. There are now 150 BTSA programs in California, and all new teachers receive 2 years of mentoring before becoming fully credentialed teachers both for those who take more traditional and those who follow alternative routes to teacher certification. Participation in such programs was previously optional, but legislative changes in 2005–2006 made it a requirement that all new teachers in California receive 2 years of mentoring.

In 2000, the SCNTP expanded to the Silicon Valley New Teacher Project, and now serves 1,000 new teachers in 30 districts. Since 1988, the SCNTP has worked with over 9,000 K–12 new teachers.

The Establishment of the New Teacher Center   In 1998, the New Teacher Center (NTC) at UCSC was founded to disseminate the lessons learned in the Santa Cruz New Teacher Project. The Center's mission is to give national scope to this work by researching, designing, and advocating for high-quality induction programs for new teachers. The NTC model is being implemented in districts across the nation as diverse as Charlotte-Mecklenburg and Durham School districts in North Carolina, the New York City public school system, the Dorchester County public school system in Maryland, an urban district in East Palo Alto, California, and rural districts in the most remote parts of Alaska, Hawaii, and Puerto Rico. The NTC is also collaborating with districts in numerous other states across the nation and consulting with other educational entities and policymakers.

The Data on Teacher Retention

As with any expenditure of scarce resources, it is important to consider the impact of such an expenditure, both on the recruitment and retention of teachers and on student achievement. Whereas national statistics suggest that only about 50% of new teachers are still in the profession after 5 years, the New Teacher Project has shown markedly better results.

The Santa Cruz New Teacher Project   A study on retention rates for new teachers supported by the SCNTP, begun in 1992, showed that, after 7 years, 88% of these teachers were still teaching in K–12 classrooms. Overall, 94% were still in some field of education. Among those interviewed, a quarter indicated that the support they had received from the SCNTP was the most important reason they had remained in the profession (Strong, 2001).

Teacher Retention in Charlotte-Mecklenburg Another study documented the impact of induction in the Charlotte-Mecklenburg schools in North Carolina in an urban district with a student body of more than 100,000. The NTC model was implemented in the most high-priority schools in the district, those in which teacher retention rates were even lower than the district as a whole. Schools in which beginning teachers received weekly mentoring found their teacher dropout rates cut almost in half. Whereas attrition rates across the district reached 32%, those schools with intensive mentoring experienced only 17.5% attrition despite the challenging nature of those sites.

Consider the Cost of Attrition Successful teacher induction programs require resources, so it is important to consider the economic benefits of increased teacher retention and whether these benefits justify the expense of induction programs. Weighing recruitment and other training costs against those of induction programs suggests that they do.

When a new teacher leaves the profession, the direct financial costs include advertising and hiring, short-term vacancy replacement, and training. The expense of losing a teacher varies, depending on the nature of the individual school. Unfortunately, schools with the highest recruitment costs are those with the highest turnover rates. In wealthy suburban schools, recruitment is comparatively inexpensive, sometimes as low as 15% of a teacher's salary, and turnover is minimal. Urban schools with a diverse population have higher recruiting expenses, which can vary between 50% and 200% of a teacher's salary, in some extreme cases (Texas Center for Education Research, 2000), and turnover tends to be much higher. For obvious reasons, it is the latter schools that benefit the most from induction programs that boost teacher retention.

With its BTSA commitment of roughly $5,700 per new teacher in the 2002–2003 school year (a combination of state- and district-level support), California spends far more on teacher retention than any another state. In a 2002 study, the California Commission on Teacher Credentialing found that the state had a retention rate of 84% after 4 years, compared to a nationwide rate of 67%. Looking at the data another way, the nation loses 33% of its teachers after 4 years, whereas California loses only 16%.

The Cost and Benefit of Induction A study of the value of induction, (Villar & Strong, 2005) yielded unexpected results. The data showed that increases in teacher effectiveness yielded greater savings than the reduction in cost associated with teacher attrition. The study suggests that an investment of $1.00 yielded a return of $1.50 at 5 years.

Key Criteria for Success in Induction

Over the evolution of the Santa Cruz New Teacher Project, the process has evolved and been refined, and a number of important lessons have been learned.

Mentor Role and Induction

Too often, in the past, mentoring programs have been merely buddy systems, in which an experienced educator is paired with a new teacher informally. In this model, mentors are neither trained for their new role nor given time to address the demands of such responsibility. In other words, new mentors are treated pretty much as new teachers were, allowed to sink or swim, armed with only intuition and good intentions to keep themselves afloat.

Effective induction programs conceive the role of mentor as "teacher of teachers." Mentors use their expertise to help support beginning teacher development in ways that are responsive to the needs of the novice teacher. This work is complex and different from teaching students. To have a real impact, induction programs must provide the same kind of support to mentors that the mentors are, in turn, providing to new teachers (Moir & Gless, 2001). Like novice teachers, new mentors need training, guidance, and the support of the entire community of educators. Even exemplary teachers need to learn new skills to be effective in sharing their wealth of experience and wisdom.

Not all good teachers make good mentors. Every mentor must have exemplary professional ability and a knowledge of standards, curriculum, and student assessment, but he or she must also demonstrate an ability to learn a new set of skills because coaching adults is very different from teaching children.

Those who are most effective are veteran teachers who have well-developed interpersonal skills. Experience with coaching, facilitating groups, and other collaborative models is an important indicator of likely success as a mentor. Successful mentors have keen observational proficiency, excellent communication skills, and, of course, patience, enthusiasm, and a love of all kinds of learning. They also must possess a commitment to collaboration and be able to build relationships, both with individuals and among groups.

Because so many new teachers are placed in schools that are culturally diverse, often with a high percentage of English-Language Learners (ELLs), special attention must be paid to hiring mentors who have experience working with diverse student populations. In such a district, ideally all new teachers are paired with mentors who have expertise in first- and second-language acquisition, literacy, and English-language development.

Mentor Professional Development

Mentoring requires new abilities: working with adults, collaboration, and, often most complex, being able to articulate the set of teaching skills that they know intuitively but rarely have been called on to communicate. Not all good teachers know how they teach; they experience their teaching practice as second nature. A good mentoring program ensures that mentors have the time and training to reflect on their practice and to collaborate with colleagues to address any concerns that arise. Effective induction programs expend time and resources to prepare mentors for their new role as communicators of their knowledge and experience. Training mentors is as important as training the novice teachers they will serve.

Mentor Training: Summer Year 1   In the SCNTP, prior to the beginning of the school year, mentor trainees participate in at least 2 days of initial training called "Foundations in Mentoring." The training covers these core areas:

- Role of the new teacher mentor
- Developing an effective mentoring relationship
- Identifying new teacher needs
- Mentoring conversations
- Formative assessment for new teachers

Mentor Training: Year 1   Throughout the year, mentors receive additional professional development, including a 2-day training in coaching and observation. This training focuses on techniques for observing new teachers, collecting classroom performance data, and using such data to inform instruction. Mentors also gather for weekly forums, which give them the opportunity to refine their mentoring skills, work collaboratively, and share insights, challenges, and successes. This learning community fosters a shared vision of good teaching, calibration of classroom observations using videos, and ability to share and analyze evidence of progress. In districts with well-established programs, these forums can help new mentors seek the guidance of those with more experience.

During the first year of mentoring, topics like these can be helpful:

- Professional teaching standards
- NTC Formative Assessment System
- Lesson planning in content areas
- Analyzing student work
- Differentiating instruction
- Collecting classroom data
- Analyzing classroom data
- Data-based revision of practice

- Effective strategies for working with English-language learners
- Literacy instruction

Mentor Training: Year 2   In the second year of a program, a new set of topics is introduced in mentor training, helping mentors to expand their roles. Experienced mentors become leaders, creating a vibrant, dynamic, and sustainable program. Typical professional development might include these components:

- Mentor professional growth
- Planning for year 2 mentoring
- Advanced coaching skills
- Promoting new teacher resiliency
- Tailoring support to second-year teachers
- Content-specific pedagogy
- Developing mentor leadership skills
- Building school-site learning communities
- Becoming a mentor trainer
- Planning for project continuation: goals and implementation plan
- Program evaluation

Many of these topics provide a forum for mentors to express their concerns and offer the leadership of the mentoring program an opportunity to assess the effectiveness of its outcomes in an informal setting. A healthy induction system is constantly gathering feedback, using the creativity and experiences of its participants to reshape itself from year to year. Programs that encourage and respond to participant feedback are more likely to sustain and enhance their effectiveness over the long term.

Mentoring Caseload and Format

Successful induction programs recognize that mentoring is an energy-consuming job, requiring time for preparation and professional development. Ideally, new teachers should have a mentor in their classroom for at least 2 hours each week, to perform demonstration lessons in the classroom, observe the novice teaching, assist with curriculum development, as well as provide guidance in classroom management and other on-the-job skills. In some districts, to meet this time commitment, mentors are released from their classroom on a full-time basis.

Dimensions of Mentoring   Not every district can afford to implement a full-release model. Some mentors combine classroom teaching with their mentoring duties. Experience has shown, however, that it is virtually impossible for teachers to spend the time and effort necessary for successful mentoring without some adjustment in scheduling. As much as possible, the mentor should be teaching the same subject(s) at the same grade levels as their mentee. This matching of content area and grade level saves the mentor valuable time and builds opportunities for deeper collaboration.

Mentor Caseload   The caseload for each mentor can be variable, depending on their experience, classroom duties, and other support available to new teachers in the district. Even experienced full-time mentors should ideally work with no more than 15 novice teachers at once. With 2 hours of classroom work per novice per week, this already represents 6 hours a day of classroom observation, assistance, and modeling. Part-time mentors, of course, cannot afford to spread themselves this thin. Without substantive weekly contact, the capacity of a mentor to contribute is greatly reduced. Simply knowing that a mentor will be in their classrooms once a week can sustain beginning teachers facing daily challenges.

Acquiring the new skills and techniques of mentoring also requires a broader time commitment. In many induction programs, mentors work with novice teachers for as long as 3 years before moving back into teaching or on to other teacher leadership roles. This extended period gives them a chance to adapt fully to their new roles. Mentors, like teachers, need time to gain their footing.

Assessment and Accountability

Statewide Standards   Induction systems operate best when both mentors and new teachers are working collaboratively toward the same goals. Professional teaching standards should be clearly defined, well articulated, and consistent statewide. In California, the *California Standards for the Teaching Profession (CSTP)* provide a framework, identifying and categorizing a set of abilities and practices that every teacher should master (California Commission on Teaching Credentialing, 1997). This provides the structure for the mentor and novice to work together to discuss progress.

Formative Assessment System   Published statewide standards are only one component of a framework for teacher growth and development. The standards then become the foundation of the Formative Assessment System (FAS), which provides structure for the interactions between mentors and beginning teachers while guiding the beginning teachers' development. Early in their first year, new teachers can be expected to work with their mentors to self-assess on the Continuum of Teacher Development by comparing their strengths and areas for growth against the benchmarks of the continuum (New Teacher Center at UCSC, 2002).

Together, they develop an Individual Learning Plan (ILP). To be useful, the process of formative assessment must also involve support for improvement, so the ILP includes a set of professional development activities designed to help the novice progress. The mentor fosters progress by collecting and discussing in-class observation data, co-developing lesson plans, making suggestions, and modeling lessons for the novice to observe.

Working together for 2 years, the mentor and novice use the ILP to share accountability. Both are responsible for maintaining a goal of high-quality teaching, constant professional inquiry, and continuous growth.

The continuity and shared responsibility of this process help the new teacher keep the ups and downs of teaching in perspective. The mentor must be seen as a trustworthy supporter and that he or she not be involved in evaluation of the new teacher. Rather than growing to fear assessment, teachers who work closely with a mentor gain the confidence to accept and implement the suggestions of their colleagues. As one new teacher in an SCNTP program said, "I meet once a week with my advisor to discuss the inevitable highs and lows. . . . She is patient and respectful, and I have learned that, most of the time, I am not so far off the track. What seems like a total derailment to me is just a minor bump. My confidence has grown."

Professional Portfolio   During these 2 years, the novice, with help from the mentor, puts together a portfolio to document progress as a teacher, including student work, observation data, and lesson plans.

Of equal importance to the assessment value of the portfolio are the benefits of the process itself. Keeping a portfolio compels beginning teachers to focus on the long term and to reflect on what they have learned. It also ensures that they develop self-assessment skills early in their careers. As one new teacher said, "The portfolio cycle has allowed me to move forward, beyond immediate needs. It has had a major impact on me, on my students, and on my collaborative team. It's the difference between being given a fish by my adviser and being taught to fish. Collaboration with an experienced teacher has enabled me to stay focused, to connect areas of practice and to reflect on my progress."

Program Assessment   Assessment is not limited, however, to the individual teachers and mentors. Each alternative route to teacher certification program should constantly work to assess its own progress, maintaining a dialogue among the leadership, the mentors, and the new teachers who are the beneficiaries of the work. Attention to such input can foster continued growth.

The most immediate forms of program assessment are surveys and interviews. The SCNTP typically conducts wide-ranging surveys of program participants at midyear and at the end of the year, collecting data from new teachers, mentors, and principals. The results are followed up with interviews of as many participants as possible.

The process of gathering feedback serves two goals. Hearing from participants helps ensure continuous program development, enabling the leadership to respond to the individual needs of the program's constituents. The feedback process also makes participants into stakeholders. When mentors and teachers have a voice in shaping the system, they gain a sense of ownership and become invested in sustaining the mentoring program in the long term.

Of course, not all program assessment is informal and anecdotal. Long-term statistical studies are also necessary to assess and understand the overall benefits of induction programs.

Mentoring and the Community

Mentoring does not reside solely in the classroom. At every step, the mentor is a collaborator, not an overseer. Mentors and new teachers work jointly to assess the new teachers' level of practice and to develop an individual plan to improve their work, including specific training activities and performance goals. The concept of collaboration goes beyond the mentor–teacher relationship; the practice of reaching out to peers, drawing on a wide network of support, and building relationships should be inculcated into every new teacher and become a career-long habit.

Professional Learning Community Whenever possible, mentors should encourage new teachers to become part of the professional community of the school. For the community to truly support them and meet their needs, novices must learn to make their voices heard. They must feel empowered to suggest curriculum innovations and new uses for technology, and to present their own solutions to day-to-day teaching challenges. After receiving new training, novices benefit from demonstrating the results to other staff members, in meetings or colloquia. New teachers should open their classrooms to visitors, to gain confidence as presenters and to feel assured that their work matters to the entire school community.

An example of such collaborative success is the Starlight Professional Development School, in the Pajaro Valley Unified School District. Starlight students are 90% Latino, and two thirds are ELLs. To help meet the communitywide need for bilingual materials, one new teacher worked with her SCNTP mentor to create a multicultural literature unit. After sharing the material with the school staff, the new teacher was invited to present her work at a summer biliteracy institute for migrant teachers. This experience of collaboration and communication moved the new teacher to say, "I feel that all of us are being trained at this school to be teacher leaders."

Collaboration among peers is also important. New teachers can meet in small groups throughout the year to brainstorm, problem-solve, and discuss issues of content and curriculum. Monthly seminars, organized at the district level and presented by mentor teachers, give new teachers a space to net-work with each other. It is important to create an atmosphere of trust that allows teachers to share and discuss successes and failures, and to make adjustments.

Collaboration with Parents and Community   Mentors can also help new teachers expand the concept of collaboration by training them in community relations. Mentors should be available to observe, assess, and model parent/teacher conferences. Veteran teachers who have worked in diverse communities can model how best to utilize knowledge of the students' multicultural backgrounds as a learning opportunity. Communities are willing to support their teachers, but activating that support takes experience that new teachers have not yet acquired. Connecting the novice to this dynamic source of assistance is a crucial role of the mentor.

Characteristics of Multidimensional Induction   This focus on collaboration and community makes induction a multidimensional process. The best induction systems are exactly that: systems. They incorporate input from new teachers, veteran teachers, administrators, unions, parents, preservice programs, and the higher educational institutions that supply educators. Communication among these groups is inherently valuable, allowing all the participants in a child's education to provide feedback and support for the new teachers on which that education depends. This feedback creates a different cycle, not one of teacher burnout and attrition, but of a cycle of ongoing development and support within the community of educators.

Summary: Key Recommendations for Induction Programs

In summary, key components of an effective induction program for candidates who are in both traditional and alternate routes to certification are that the program is sufficiently funded and uses proven methodologies, has stakeholder support, and generally includes the following core elements:

- *Full-time program administrators*   Programs should be staffed with innovative, full-time program administrators with the training, time, and resources to establish and run excellent programs.
- *Quality mentoring*   Mentoring should take place during the school day, in class and one on one, with sanctioned time for both mentors and beginning teachers.
- *Mentor selection*   Mentors should be selected for their ability to work with adults, their expertise in pedagogy and content areas, their leadership qualities, and their commitment to collaborative work.
- *Mentor development*   A mentor needs ongoing training and support to be the most effective "teacher of teachers."
- *Formative assessment for beginning teachers*   New teachers, with help from their mentors, should systematically identify areas for growth, set personal performance goals, and develop the skills needed to attain these goals.

- *Training in data collection and analysis* New teachers and mentors should be trained to collect classroom data, analyze data, and use the results to guide instruction.
- *Training for site administrators* Site administrators must understand the needs of beginning teachers, provide them with resources, and learn techniques for evaluation that build teacher practice.
- *Teaching standards* New teacher guidance and self-assessment must take into account the accepted state standards for what teachers need to know and be able to do.
- *High expectations for new teachers, mentors, and students* Induction programs should be expected to help teachers excel, not just survive.
- *Training for work with diverse students and English-language learners* Additional support is necessary for areas with minority students and English learners because beginning teachers are frequently placed in schools serving these students (Peske & Haycock, 2006).
- *Networking and training opportunities for beginning teachers* Workshops and training sessions help novices overcome the traditional isolation of teachers.
- *Contractually bargained new teacher placement* Working with teacher unions, policymakers should ensure that new teachers are not routinely placed with the hardest-to-serve students in high-priority schools.

This is not a list from which to pick and choose, but rather a coherent approach for effective change. Each of these elements is important, and each has been shown to support the others, creating a well-rounded robust system that has the capacity to transform the experience of a teacher's first years and to engage their experienced colleagues in the process. The multidimensional aspect of this work, incorporating new and veteran teachers, administrators, unions, and parents, is capable of not only solving a crisis in teacher hiring but of transforming the culture of education in the United States.

To implement a program with these levels of support requires resources. A system of quality teacher induction costs money, but compared with the financial expense and educational cost of recruiting and training replacements, the cost of effective induction is relatively low. In California, under BTSA, in 2005–2006 the state provided nearly $3,500 for each new teacher, and districts were required to contribute at least another $2,000. Levels of $5,000 and $6,000 per new teacher have proven adequate for a top-flight system of induction.

With these realities in mind, it is very important that when states mandate induction programs they also provide adequate funding to help districts meet these mandates. Mentoring is not a cost-free process. It is, however, a proven and effective system that requires a serious commitment of resources at both the state and district levels.

Establishing an Induction Program

To establish a vibrant induction program, there are a number of steps to consider. Working with a team to address and resolve the issues described here will allow you to build stakeholder buy-in and to create a program tailored to the needs of your particular context.

Identifying and Enlisting Support of Stakeholders

The most successful induction programs are established with the support of all the parties who may be impacted by the program. This includes, but is not limited to, state policymakers, regional and local district administrators, site administrators, superintendents and principals, veteran teachers, teachers' unions, and possibly others, such as preservice educators. It is generally helpful to explore what local universities are doing both in terms of preservice instruction and in terms of continuing education for teachers. It is vital to ensure that all those who will be impacted by such a program, and who may impact such a program, are included from the start, to avoid problems later. Time spent in educating and enlisting support from these individuals will enhance the effectiveness of the development program and can pay dividends over the long term. Ideally, you would then establish a working group, which can become the steering committee for the new induction program.

Exploring the Context

Once these individuals are informed about induction, they can then move on to a discussion of issues that relate to how induction might be undertaken within the local context of the alternate routes to teacher certification. Consideration should be given to what challenges and opportunities might exist. They might wish to reflect on whether there are any structural hurdles they face and whether there are any timing issues that might impact such a program. Consideration should also be given to what professional development initiatives and resources are available and what has or has not worked in the past. Sometimes induction efforts fail, not because of the quality of the work that has been done, but rather because they haven't effectively engaged the support of all the stakeholders who view change as threatening to the status quo.

It is important to ensure that all participants are heard, and that, from the start, an atmosphere supportive of discourse and dialogue is established. Likewise, it is helpful if participants in such a process develop a common set of definitions and concepts to avoid miscommunication.

Identifying Governing Standards

There are a number of different kinds of standards that may be in place and that states use to guide such work. These will be particular to each state, although they may or may not exist.

Teaching Standards   The group must build consensus on what is best practice in teaching and understand the local and state regulatory context of such work. This is most effective in states where there are established professional standards for the teaching profession. In states that do not have such standards, it may be helpful to review what other states have used as the basis of discussion.

Program Standards   Some states have established program standards either for induction in general or for specific settings. For example, Virginia has program standards to be used for mentoring programs in hard-to-staff schools. Such standards address the issues comparable to those addressed in an induction plan, such as these:

- Program design
- Sponsorship, administration, and leadership
- Resources
- Coordination and communication
- Mentor teacher selection and assignment
- Mentor teacher training professional development
- Roles and responsibilities of K–12 schools
- Individual learning plan
- Formative assessment system
- Evaluation

Professional Development Standards   Some states also have standards for teacher professional development either as part of the teacher certification legislation, as part of the state regulatory process, or as part of agreements with the local teachers' unions. These, too, must be considered.

Issues related to Standards   In many states that have standards, these standards have not been developed simultaneously. Thus, the team must review these documents and determine where they are incongruent and identify how they plan to address such issues.

Evaluation of Essential Program Components

The next step in the process is to reach consensus on the status of a number of aspects of the proposed program. For each of these aspects, it is helpful to discuss and identify the strengths, challenges, opportunities, and threats.

As you review these, consider all aspects in the time frame of the program from its inception, development, and implementation through its integration and into subsequent evaluation and refinement.

Program Vision   This conversation should include consideration of objectives of the program. Are we trying to:

- enhance recruitment?
- improve retention?
- impact student achievement?
- increase teacher quality?
- influence the career path for exemplary veteran teachers?

Any such conversation should include review, not only of the objectives of those in the room, but the potential priorities of others such as funding sources and administrators who will impact the implementation and evaluation of the project. Successful induction programs routinely credit support from district administration as a key contributor to the success of the program.

Institutional Commitment and Support   One must evaluate all aspects of buy-in from those who are stakeholders. One should make a realistic evaluation of opportunities and possible impediments to progress.

Quality Mentoring   Here again, it is important to reach consensus on what is meant by "quality mentoring" and assess what will influence your success in achieving such a program.

Professional Standards   How will aspects of state professional standards impact the formation and implementation of such a program? Are your standards well drafted, and will they provide a useful basis for induction?

Classroom-Based Teacher Learning   It is useful to have agreement on the status of teaching in your school. How good are the students' test scores? Are they improving over time? Are there underserved groups? What additional resources are available, such as literacy coaches?

Induction Program Norms

Any new program can benefit from explicit consideration of norms. One of the dilemmas often faced by mentors is that administrators may look to them to evaluate their mentee, whereas the mentoring relationship is most effective as a trust relationship where the mentor is an advocate for the new teacher. A positive supportive environment fosters development of a situation where both novice and veteran teachers are willing to take chances, secure that they will not be judged. One must evaluate whether there are existing cultural issues that can threaten establishment of a such an atmosphere and consider what might be done to address such an issue.

Use of a Formative Assessment System

As discussed earlier, the NTC induction program is founded in the use of a Formative Assessment System. Such an approach not only supports the use of standards to help a new teacher move along a learning continuum, but it also fosters an approach to self-assessment and reflection that the teacher can use for ongoing improvement throughout his or her career. In reviewing the possible approaches, consider the following factors.

Support for Formative Assessment   What do we already have in place that supports the use of professional standards and formative assessment practice? How can existing resources be enhanced?

Existing Resources   What connections already exist between current beginning teacher support efforts and local professional development and/or evaluation processes?

New Opportunities   What additional connections might be possible, in your context, to support the use of professional standards and formative assessment practices? How might one enlist such resources as these:

- Local staff development
- Evaluation systems/practices
- Site initiatives
- Preservice programs
- Other

Examples of Successful Induction Programs

This section provides examples of how several districts across the nation have implemented exemplary induction programs, and then it outlines possible sources of funding.

Induction Program in Durham, North Carolina   The induction program in Durham was launched in 2005–2006. Durham supports new teachers for the first 3 years of their practice and almost a quarter of the teachers are eligible. Mentors are full release and have a caseload of 20 novice teachers, of whom 15 are in the first 2 years of teaching, and the other 5 are third-year teachers who require substantially less support.

The program was launched with a 3-year, $100,000 per year grant from the Duke Foundation to cover the cost of starting the program and training the mentors. The cost of funding the support for the mentors is about $2,868 per new teacher, including all 3 years, or about $3,824 per new teacher for those in the first 2 years of practice. It is comprised of 55% federal, Title II funds, 14% state funds, and 31% local funds, which includes some funding for high-priority schools.

Induction Program in Mapleton, Colorado   Mapleton is a small district with 13 schools and 339 teachers, including 60 to 100 beginning teachers. The district has implemented a program with four full-release mentors, three in general education and one with skills in special education, each of whom support 12 to 18 new teachers. Their mentors are all veteran teachers who are close to retirement and would prefer to continue to mentor rather than return to the classroom.

The start-up training for mentors was originally funded by a Carnegie TIPS grant. The district and Title II funds have always paid for the salaries of the mentors and the rest of the induction program. The program currently costs about $199,000 per year, or about $3,100 per beginning teacher. About 69% of the funding comes from Title II and the remaining 31% is from general district funds, which include both local and state sponsorship.

District leaders believe the program has been extremely successful, and they have reduced the turnover rate, although they would like to reduce it further. The key to the success in continuing the program and the funding is the fact that the superintendent is extremely supportive and believes the program is a priority for the district.

Induction Program in Amherst, Virginia   Amherst is a small district with about 450 teachers and 4,700 students in ten schools—one high school, two middle schools, and seven elementary schools—and is at the end of the seventh year of its induction program. The New Teacher Center Induction Model was added to the ACPS Program during the 2003–2004 school year. In 2004–2005, the novice was mentored for only the first year of teaching, and 29 mentors supported 31 new teachers. This year there were only 24 new teachers. Next year the program will be expanded to include those in the second year of teaching, and there will be 46 mentors. It is a model that allows for at least a couple of hours a week of release time and provides the mentors a $1,000 stipend. The mentors are in the same school as their mentees but not necessarily in the same subject area or grade.

The district uses a continuum based on the one for California but tailored to the Virginia Teaching Standards. They have coordinated with several local IHEs in the area: Sweetbriar, Randolph Macon, and Lynchburg. The preservice programs train students on the use of the continuum, so it provides a seamless transition to the induction program.

At the same time, this district has been involved in a differentiation project, based on the work of Carol Tomlinson, for several years. Three elementary schools, one middle school, and the high school are involved, and they have 3 all-day seminars addressing how to apply the theory, analysis of student work, and the impact on lesson planning. The mentors involved in this project coach new and veteran teachers in this process and model effective application of the program.

The induction program has been very successful in helping the district attract and retain new teachers. This year only four teachers left; two were not invited back, one moved to get married, and one enrolled in a master's program. All the major stakeholders have recognized the contribution of the induction program, and the school administration is committed to finding ongoing funding to continue the work. The mentors are very engaged in the work, and a number of them are pursuing National Board Certification.

The initial start-up expenses were covered by a 2-year $100,000 grant from the Virginia Department of Education. The ongoing expenses, such as teacher stipends; substitutes, so participants can attend training, model, and observe in classrooms; materials; and trainings are funded about 25% from Title II funds and the balance comes from the district. This is a comparatively inexpensive program, costing about $2,800 per new teacher.

Funding Induction

One of the most common concerns expressed about induction is whether a district can afford to fund the program.

Federal Resources   Currently, most induction program funding begins with federal resources. Title IIA, Teacher Quality money, often provides a substantial portion of the resources. In 2006, this program was allocated over $2.8 billion, and the U.S. Department of Education (DoE) anticipates funding 57 new programs. Title I may have funds for low-performing schools. In addition, one can go to the DoE Website (see the links at the end of this book) and find a variety of other programs that might provide the basis for such an approach. For example, a rural district might find money in CFDA 84.358A, which authorizes funding to local education authorities (LEAs) to carry out work authorized in other federal programs.

Funding for alternate certification includes Transition to Teaching, a DoE initiative to support alternate certification. The Adjunct Teacher Corps: Bringing Real World Experience into the Classroom encourages math, science, and foreign language professionals to teach at the secondary school level. Troops to Teachers is a U.S. Department of Education and Department of Defense program that helps eligible military personnel begin new careers as teachers in public schools where their skills, knowledge, and experience are most needed.

CFDA 84.286 Ready to Teach has funding for innovative programs to improve teaching in core curriculum areas and support innovative educational and instructional video programming. CFDA 84.283B, Office of School Support and Technology Programs, is designed to provide grants to help low-performing schools close achievement gaps.

CFDA 84.336 is targeted at programs for improving teacher preparation and teacher recruitment, which might be structured to include induction, but only a few states have remaining eligibility. The U.S. Department of Commerce has funding under the Workforce Investment Act, which has been used by some districts to support induction in poor high-need communities.

Other special programs exist, such as those for English-Language Learners, Native Americans, technology, and so on, all of which can be considered as you design a program that will meet the needs of your program and also match the specifications of funding programs. There is ongoing federal interest in funding specific content areas, such as math and science. Such resources could help address the needs of one or more mentors in these fields within a district.

Do not anticipate that a program will be supported by a single source. Rather, expect to cobble together a variety of resources to arrive at a solution. As you read through the purpose and eligibility requirements, review the current funding status and determine when the program is scheduled to sunset, to be sure that such a program will still be available when you need it.

Federal funds are also available to states in the form of categorical funds given to the states as block grants. Again, use of such resources vary by state, but it is important to explore and understand priorities for such funds in your state and to identify and exploit funding windows of opportunity.

State Funds States, too, often have funds available for objectives such as professional development and reducing class size. These may be made available systematically or may require a proposal to be made with an outline of a program included. Again, local funds may allow for some forms of induction, although the problem is often that the district is required to make trade-offs between programs that are important to different constituencies.

Other Resources There are also other possibilities for creative approaches. In some instances, districts have partnered with local university education departments to smooth the transition from preservice to inservice, and these partnerships can be effective in obtaining grant funding. In other instances, local foundations have been willing to fund a pilot program in induction or to fund a portion of induction on an ongoing basis. You might also consider contacting local corporations, which can be helpful in supporting the program, either with materials such as computers, with meeting space, or with other resources.

You might also want to explore online resources. In California, districts are putting their professional development courses, designed to meet state legislative requirements, online so the district makes a token fee and other districts can benefit from the work they have done. In addition, there are programs such as the one through the National Science Foundation (NSF) and the National Science Teachers' Association designed to support new math and science teachers online.

Developing a Plan

Having reviewed and considered the aspects of induction, the next step is to reconsider and document your program. In each aspect of the program, take into account, and specify, your objective(s).

Then you must revisit each section to specify what the next steps are to reach those objectives, who will be responsible for taking those next steps, and to set a target date when those tasks will be completed. It may be helpful to map out a timeline, which will reflect any tasks that need to precede other projects and any tasks where individuals have overlapping responsibilities that will impact the completion date. As in any project, it is helpful to build in contingency time for unforeseen circumstances and to identify a person or group that will shepherd the project as it evolves. You can also define milestones, where the group will stop, reevaluate progress, and identify opportunities to be more effective.

Your plan should include consideration of the following:

1. *Program Design and Goals*
   What sort of induction program do we want to create?
   What impact do we seek?
   Who is responsible for what?
   How are we ensuring our program impacts student outcomes?
   What professional norms do we intend to establish?

2. *Program Administration*
   Who is responsible for administering the program?
   What additional linkages can support our induction program?
   How can we build strong ongoing stakeholder support?
   What kind of organizational meetings will we need, with what frequency, and when?

3. *Funding*
   What are our funding sources?
   How can we build a sustainable budgetary infrastructure?
   What linkages will support this infrastructure?

4. *Mentor Selection*
   How will we recruit and select mentors?
   What are our selection criteria?
   Who are our potential mentors?
   What sort of mentor model do we want to create?
   What coordination with unions or others will be required?

5. *Mentor Role*

How will our mentors work with beginning teachers?
What structures/resources can support the mentors?
What will be the mentor caseload?
How will mentors meet individual teachers' needs?
How will mentors be held accountable for their work?

6. *Mentor Development*

How will we support our mentors?
What do our mentors need to know and be able to do?
What sort of professional development will we offer our mentors?
Who will offer ongoing professional development for mentors?

7. *Beginning Teacher Participation*

How will beginning teachers be solicited and selected for participation?
What structures will help differentiate support in response to beginning teachers' varying needs?
How will beginning teachers be held accountable?

8. *Beginning Teacher Professional Development*

What sort of professional development will we offer our beginning teachers?
What will our orientation include? When will it occur?
How will we build beginning teacher commitment to the program?
What role can an institute for higher education play?

9. *Equitable Student Learning*

How will we support mentors and new teachers' focus on equitable student learning?
What does closing the achievement gap mean in our context?
What are key strategies/approaches for novice teachers?
How can we build mentor and supervisor capacity around issues of equity?

10. *Formative Assessment*

How will mentors assess beginning teachers so they provide the most appropriate support?
What tools and structures will we use?
How will we support our mentors and beginning teachers in using these tools effectively?
How might formative assessment tools be used in preservice?

11. *Program Evaluation*

What outcomes do we hope to achieve?
How and how often will we measure our progress?
What data and documentation can support our program review?
What help or guidance do we need?
Who will oversee program evaluation?

12. *Preservice*

How will we link induction practices with preservice?

How will we support this alignment?

What institution of higher education resources, policies, or practices support these efforts?

Conclusion: A New Dimension of Teaching

Experience has shown that mentoring has an immediate and practical effect on the professional lives of new teachers and their students. Quality induction programs result in greater teacher retention, breaking the cycle of attrition, which in turn saves money for school districts and ensures that teacher shortages do not dictate hiring policy. These benefits are felt most in those school districts most affected by attrition where students come from a background of poverty and cultural or linguistic diversity. These are the districts with the highest turnover and the greatest replacement costs; these are also the districts where participants in programs offering alternative routes to teacher certification are needed.

Mentoring can also have a profound effect on our system of education, not only fostering the practice of the novice but also transforming the careers of exemplary veteran teachers. Mentors often find themselves revitalized by the experience of passing their knowledge on to a new generation of teachers. Some mentors return to the classroom after a few years and discover that they have gained a broader perspective on teaching and learning. Many become "teacher leaders" in their schools, using the mentoring skills they have learned in an informal capacity to foster the work of their colleagues and departments, continuing to nurture this professional growth in their local community of educators. Other mentors go on to administrative positions using their newly learned leadership skills to become successful principals and administrators. Those who enter administration take with them both a well-rounded understanding of new teacher needs and hands-on experience with professional development.

All these benefits reflect the fact that mentoring transforms the teaching profession from an atmosphere of isolation and high turnover to one of collaboration, continuity, and community. Learning to teach continues well beyond training and preservice and becomes a process that extends across an entire career. Mentoring cultivates productive interaction among generations of teachers, creating an environment in which experience is valued, creativity rewarded, and professional satisfaction is nurtured.

A quality induction system can sustain and nourish that initial enthusiasm the new teacher brings on his or her first day. It can also serve to reinvigorate veteran teachers, foster development of teacher leaders, improve student achievement, and impact the ongoing approach to continuous improvement within the entire school.

Useful Links

U.S. Department of Education frequently asked questions (FAQs) and current grant programs, including information on current programs, programs that are forecast to be funded, and other government programs, are linked from the following page:

http://www.ed.gov/fund/grant/find/edpicks.jhtml?src=ln.
To receive updates on DoE programs go to

http://www.ed.gov/news/newsletters/edinfo/index.html?src=ln.
Information on Transition to Teaching funding is available at

http://www.ed.gov/programs/transitionteach/resourcesarc.html.
For Adjunct Teacher Corps: Bringing Real World Experience into the Classroom, visit

http://www.ed.gov/about/inits/ed/competitiveness/teachercorps.html.

References

Achinstein, B., & Athanases, S. (2006). *Mentors in the making: Developing new leaders for new teachers.* New York: Teachers College Press.

California Commission on Teaching Credentialing. (1997). *California standards for the teaching profession.* Sacramento, CA: Author.

Fulton, K., Yoon, I., & Lee, C. (2005). *Induction into learning communities.* National Commission on Teaching and America's Future.

Moir, E., & Gless, J. (2001). Quality induction: An investment in teachers. *Teacher Education Quarterly, 28,*(1), 109–114.

New Teacher Center at UCSC. (2002). *Continuum of teacher development.* Santa Cruz, CA: ToucanEd.

No dream denied. (2003). Report of the National Commission on Teaching and America's Future. Washington, DC: The National Commission on Teaching and America's Future.

Peske, H. G., & Haycock, K. (2006). *Teaching inequality: How poor and minority students are shortchanged on teacher quality.* Washington, DC: The Education Trust.

Smith, T. M., & Ingersoll, R. M. (2004). What are the effects of induction and mentoring on beginning teacher turnover? *American Educational Research Journal, 41*(3), 681–714.

Strong, M. (2001). A study of teacher retention: The effects of mentoring for beginning teachers. Retrieved from www.newteachercenter.org.

Texas Center for Education Research. (2000). *The cost of teacher turnover.* Prepared for the Texas State Board for Educator Certification, Austin.

Villar, A., & Strong, M. (2005). Is mentoring worth the money? A benefit-cost analysis and five year rate of return of a comprehensive mentoring program for beginning teachers. Manuscript submitted for publication.

4

Standards-Based
Curriculum Development:
One Program's Journey

Becky Washington

Texas Region XIII

*T*he Education Service Center Region XIII's Educator Certification
Program (ECP) in Austin, Texas, was one of six alternative certification
programs studied for highlighting in the booklet *Alternative Routes to Teacher
Certification,* published by the U.S. Department of Education's Office of
Innovation and Improvement. In the summary of this program, the DoE
listed the Texas program's alignment of the curriculum with state academic
and performance standards as one of its strengths. The alignment of the
Region XIII ECP's curriculum with state standards was a long process that
required much planning, many "restarts," and a great deal of perseverance.

The design of Region XIII's ECP has some unique features that are important in understanding the curriculum design. Participants are required to
make an 1.5-year investment in the program. The teacher-candidates, or
interns, begin preservice training in January by participating in online facili-
tated coursework intended to address the "highly qualified" component of
the *No Child Left Behind* (NCLB) legislation. The Texas Education Agency has
ruled that no teacher may be recommended for a probationary certificate (the
certificate used for participants in alternative certification programs while
preparing for their standard certificate) until he or she has met the highly
qualified component. These interns, therefore, spend approximately
10 weeks in online coursework developing or improving their content knowledge to enable them to pass the rigorous state content exams, which are taken
in the spring, usually April. This schedule gives participants plenty of time to
secure a teaching position by August when their internship begins.

The online coursework was created by Region XIII staff and master teachers throughout the 16-county region. ECP staff reviewed it to confirm that it aligned with the state standards, and they provided the training necessary for candidates to pass the state content exam.

In mid-March, all participants begin a blended model (both online and face to face) of training that focuses on the content required to pass the Pedagogy and Professional Responsibilities (PPR) state exam. Region XIII ECP chose a blended model of delivery based on the philosophy that some pedagogical concepts are best learned through modeling, practicing, and discussing. Pieces of the curriculum that are primarily an acquisition of knowledge were developed as online modules. Parts needing modeling, practice with supervision, or unpacking, as it were, through ongoing discussion were developed in a face-to-face model of delivery. Because the curriculum is based on state requirements, the units of study come directly from the Texas standards and fall into four domains: designing instruction, classroom environment, delivering instruction, and professional roles and responsibilities.

Interns participate in preservice training through the end of July, which includes a 2-week field experience in late April and early May. During the field experience, the interns practice in a classroom setting the concepts they learned in their preservice training. They then begin their internship in August. However, the internship is more than simply the first year of teaching. The interns continue their training in the same four areas just listed: designing instruction, classroom environment, delivering instruction, and professional roles and responsibilities. Some of the inservice training spirals back to concepts introduced in preservice; however, more depth of understanding can occur during this time because the interns are coming to training straight from their classrooms and going right back into their classrooms. This allows them to put into practice immediately what they are learning during inservice. The ECP instructors add other concepts based on what they learn by observing the interns in their classrooms.

Region XIII ECP began the curriculum alignment and development process in 2002, anticipating a year-long process. However, the planners have continued fine-tuning the curriculum over the last 4 years, with the most recent changes completed in 2006. It is this 4-year-long process that has enabled the program to achieve the characteristics and outcomes deemed critical to teacher and student success.

Many pieces of the certification process affect whether or not a teacher-candidate becomes an effective lifelong teacher. Some of these are out of the control of the certification program. For instance, in their report *Characteristics of Effective Alternative Teacher Certification Programs*, Humphrey, Wechsler, and Hough (2005) state that the placement of teachers during their first year of teaching is critical to their success and retention in the profession. However, this is often not within the control of the certification program. Other factors, including the innate abilities that the teacher brings to the profession, such as commitment, dedication, or positivity, are also not within the control of the certification program.

Humphrey et al. (2005) state, "[O]ur evidence suggests that an effective alternative certification program should have a carefully crafted and well-timed sequence of coursework that is relevant to the challenges facing alternative certified teachers" (p. 40). Why has Region XIII ECP put so much time and emphasis on their curriculum development? The program believes that this "carefully crafted and well-timed sequence of coursework" is the one thing totally within the control of the certification program and critical to the success of their interns.

Sometimes, however, it may seem as if the staff of the certification program is looking into a deep dark hole as they try to determine how to put that sequence of coursework together. What can make the sequencing seem so murky are the many available options along with the many opinions about what constitutes best practice. For example, some teacher educators are convinced that learning the history of public education is a crucial part of the curriculum. But many certification programs do not teach this at all and see it as irrelevant. Then there are the multiple options within courses. Within the realm of classroom management are many models or theories about what is best practice. Which one, then, should a program choose?

This chapter shares the journey one certification program took to make certain the curriculum prepared for their interns could be considered a viable, guaranteed curriculum, as defined by Marzano (2003) in *What Works in Schools*, a curriculum that ensures each intern receives the same information to the same depth with the same assurance of understanding. Another measure of success was that the interns who completed the coursework based on this curriculum showed improved student achievement in their classrooms.

Why Curriculum?

Purpose of Curriculum

When beginning their journey, the Region XIII staff first had to develop some important understandings about curriculum. They believed curriculum provides the foundation to give aspiring teachers the knowledge and skills they need to be successful, effective educators. The delivery of curriculum can either enhance or deter the acquisition of those knowledge and skills. In this chapter, the discussion primarily focuses on the program's selection of the curriculum, with minimal discussion of curriculum delivery.

As the discussion continues, however, it will become apparent that it is almost impossible to separate one from the other. A good analogy might be a musical performance. The musical score provides the framework, or road map, for a great musical experience. The delivery by the instrumentalists can enhance or detract from the score. The same is true of curriculum. A good curriculum provides the framework, but the teaching staff's delivery can enhance or detract from it. The opposite is also true. Just as it is almost impossible for a great orchestra to make a poorly written musical score sound wonderful, it is also difficult for even a great teacher to be successful with a poorly written curriculum. The foundational element of doing a great job of selecting and developing the curriculum can go a long way toward assuring its effectiveness, regardless of the delivery.

Selecting an Appropriate Curriculum

Multiple Options

As the Region XIII ECP staff began to redevelop the program's curriculum, they discovered that certification programs use a variety of methods for selecting curriculum. Within their own program, they found that some of the existing curriculum was there because of historical trends: "That's the way we've always done it." Sometimes it was the personal preference of an individual staff member—"Differentiation of instruction is my passion." Sometimes it was the need to correct past errors—"Our participants regularly performed poorly in this area," or "Our teachers frequently used this skill poorly in their classrooms." And sometimes the curriculum was based on the needs or initiatives of the school districts served by the program—"This is the reading program used by our largest hiring district."

Considered individually, none of these criteria provide a consistent, effective methodology for selecting, developing, or sustaining curriculum. Historical trends have not necessarily kept up with new research. Personal preference is not necessarily backed by solid research. In correcting past errors, new errors could be made. Bowing to the initiatives of specific districts could leave out the needs of other districts.

Researchers and practitioners nationwide have developed sets of standards around the knowledge and skills that novice teachers need. Those standards are based on research that links them to measures of efficacy in teaching performance, retention in the field, and student outcomes. Most states have either adopted these or have used them as a basis for writing their own standards. By relying on these state or national standards as the basis for curriculum, we can be reasonably assured that there will be a "carefully crafted and well-timed sequence of coursework that is relevant to the challenges facing alternative certified teachers," as stated by Humphrey et al (2005, p. 40). Just as in the musical performance, the quality of the performance is more reasonably assured when the score is well crafted.

Best Practice Bases the Curriculum on Standards

Purpose of Standards   By dictionary definition, a standard is "something established by authority, custom, or general consent as a model or example; a criterion." We might question why it would be necessary to have standards for teacher candidates as well as why it might be considered best practice to base curriculum on standards. To understand this, the Region XIII staff looked at their state standards and studied the process that brought about those standards.

Sources of Standards   The Interstate New Teacher Assessment and Support Consortium (INTASC) is a group of state education agencies and national educational organizations dedicated to the reform of the preparation, licensing, and ongoing professional development of teachers. It is a project of the Council of Chief State School Officers (CCSSO). In a 1992 report, INTASC (1992) noted,

> Efforts to restructure America's schools for the demands of a knowledge-based economy are redefining the mission of schooling and the job of teaching. Rather than merely "offering education," schools are now expected to ensure that all students learn and perform at high levels. Rather than merely "covering the curriculum," teachers are expected to find ways to support and connect with the needs of all learners. This new mission requires substantially more knowledge and skill of teachers and more student-centered approaches to organizing schools. These learner-centered approaches to teaching and schooling require, in turn, supportive policies for preparing, licensing, and certifying educators and for regulating and accrediting schools. (p. 5)

CCSSO states on its Website,

> INTASC believes that all education policy should be driven by what we want our P–12 students to know and be able to do. Thus, all aspects of a state's education system should be aligned with and organized to achieve the state's policy as embodied in its P–12 student standards. This includes its teacher licensing system. Teacher licensing standards are the state's policy for what all teachers must know and be able to do in order to effectively help all students achieve the P–12 student standards. The teacher licensing standards become the driving force behind how a state's teacher licensing system (program approval, licensing assessments, professional development) is organized and implemented. (www.ccsso.org)

Table 4.1   INTASC Standards

Principle 1:   The teacher understands the central concepts, tools of inquiry, and structures of the discipline(s) he or she teaches and can create learning experiences that make these aspects of subject matter meaningful for students.

Principle 2:   The teacher understands how children learn and develop, and can provide learning opportunities that support their intellectual, social, and personal development.

Principle 3:   The teacher understands how students differ in their approaches to learning and creates instructional opportunities that are adapted to diverse learners.

Principle 4:   The teacher understands and uses a variety of instructional strategies to encourage students' development of critical thinking, problem solving, and performance skills.

Principle 5:   The teacher uses an understanding of individual and group motivation and behavior to create a learning environment that encourages positive social interaction, active engagement in learning, and self-motivation.

Principle 6:   The teacher uses knowledge of effective verbal, nonverbal, and media communication techniques to foster active inquiry, collaboration, and supportive interaction in the classroom.

Principle 7:   The teacher plans instruction based upon knowledge of subject matter, students, the community, and curriculum goals.

Principle 8:   The teacher understands and uses formal and informal assessment strategies to evaluate and ensure the continuous intellectual, social, and physical development of the learner.

Principle 9:   The teacher is a reflective practitioner who continually evaluates the effects of his/her choices and actions on others (students, parents, and other professionals in the learning community) and who actively seeks out opportunities to grow professionally.

Principle 10: The teacher fosters relationships with school colleagues, parents, and agencies in the larger community to support students' learning and well-being.

Source: The Interstate New Teacher Assessment and Support Consortium (INTASC) standards were developed by the Council of Chief State School Officers and member states. Copies may be downloaded from the Council's website at http:www.ccsso.org.

As a result, INTASC has articulated standards for a common core of teaching knowledge and skills that should be acquired by all new teachers, as shown in Table 4.1. In Table 4.3, an example shows how each standard is followed by knowledge, performance, and disposition indicators that further delineate each standard.

Charlotte Danielson (1996), while working with the Educational Testing Service (ETS), developed a framework for state and local agencies

Table 4.2   Framework for Teaching Components

Domain 1: Planning and Preparation	Domain 2: The Classroom Environment
• 1a: Demonstrating Knowledge of Content and Pedagogy • 1b: Demonstrating Knowledge of Students • 1c: Selecting Instructional Goals • 1d: Demonstrating Knowledge of Resources • 1e: Designing Coherent Instruction • 1f: Assessing Student Learning	• 2a: Creating an Environment of Respect and Rapport • 2b: Establishing a Culture for Learning • 2c: Managing Classroom Procedures • 2d: Managing Student Behavior • 2e: Organizing Physical Space
Domain 3: Instruction	Domain 4: Professional Responsibilities
• 3a: Communicating Clearly and Accurately • 3b: Using Questioning and Discussion Techniques • 3c: Engaging Students in Learning • 3d: Providing Feedback to Students • 3e: Demonstrating Flexibility and Responsiveness	• 4a: Reflecting on Teaching • 4b: Maintaining Accurate Records • 4c: Communicating with Families • 4d: Contributing to the School and District • 4e: Growing and Developing Professionally • 4f: Showing Professionalism

Source: Danielson, C. (2007). *Enhancing Professional Practice: A Framework for Teaching,* Second Edition. Alexandria, VA: Association for Supervision and Curriculum Development.

to use in making decisions about the licensing of teachers. This framework set up four domains, each containing components of what is required of the teacher candidate (see Table 4.2). Danielson also developed the indicators that further describe each component. To assess domain mastery, ETS created the *Praxis Series: Professional Assessments for Beginning Teachers.*

These efforts to create learner-centered standards for teachers, although somewhat different, are very much compatible with one another. For example, principle 5 of the INTASC standards is comparable to domain 2 in the ETS Framework (see Table 4.3). The table also shows how the INTASC standards are broken down into knowledge, disposition, and performance standards. In her book *Enhancing Professional Practice: A Framework for Teaching,* Danielson (1996) compares these two sets of standards (pp. 10–11).

Many states have used either the INTASC standards or the ETS Framework as a basis for their educator standards. Understanding standards and the indicators attached to them was the first step the Region XIII staff took in putting together a carefully crafted and well-timed sequence of coursework.

Table 4.3   Comparison of INTASC and Danielson Framework

Principle 5: The teacher uses an understanding of individual and group motivation and behavior to create a learning environment that encourages positive social interaction, active engagement in learning, and self-motivation.

- **Knowledge:**
  K1.The teacher can use knowledge about human motivation and behavior drawn from the foundational sciences of psychology, anthropology, and sociology to develop strategies for organizing and supporting individual and group work.
  K2.The teacher understands how social groups function and influence people, and how people influence groups.

- **Dispositions**
  D1.The teacher takes responsibility for establishing a positive climate in the classroom and participates in maintaining such a climate in the school as a whole.
  D2.The teacher understands how participation supports commitment, and is committed to the expression and use of democratic values in the classroom.

- **Performances**
  P1.The teacher creates a smoothly functioning learning community in which students assume responsibility for themselves and one another, participate in decision making, work collaboratively and independently, and engage in purposeful learning activities.
  P2.The teacher engages students in individual and cooperative learning activities that help them develop the motivation to achieve by, for example, relating lessons to students' personal interests, allowing students to have choices in their learning, and leading students to ask questions and pursue problems that are meaningful to them.

Domain 2: The Classroom Environment
- 2a: Creating an Environment of Respect and Rapport
- 2b: Establishing a Culture for Learning
- 2c: Managing Classroom Procedures
- 2d: Managing Student Behavior
- 2e: Organizing Physical Space

Note: Not all knowledge, disposition, and performance states have been included for this INTASC principle.

Source: INTASC standards adapted from www.org/content/pdfs/corestrd.pdf. Danielson Framework adapted from Danielson, C. (2007). *Enhancing Professional Practice: A Framework for Teaching*, Second Edition. Alexandria, VA: Association for Supervision and Curriculum Development.

Within Standards, Deciding What to Teach

Use of Standards

Once the Region XIII staff was well versed in the requirements and standards for their state, the next difficult step was determining how to use those standards. In his book *Making Standards Work*, Douglas B. Reeves (2002) states,

> Standards implementation inevitably leads to curriculum reform. . . . If standards are to become more than a slogan, then one of two things must happen. Either the classes that are not associated with standards are no longer taught, or . . . the teachers of those classes creatively identify ways their classes can help students achieve academic standards. (p. 12)

Sometimes it may be easier to start fresh in developing curriculum aligned to standards than to try to rework or retool the current curriculum content creatively to make it align to standards. This was the case at Region XIII when it aligned its curriculum to the Texas standards.

Curriculum Audits

A new certification program likely starts with a blank slate in curriculum development. If they are not contracting with a local university or with professional developers, staff have the opportunity to take the appropriate standards and mold them into curriculum units without the baggage of previously developed curriculum. However, people using established certification programs may wonder why they ever need to address their curriculum. Some of the staff at the Region XIII program made this type of statement. To make sure the curriculum design project was the direction the program needed to take, the staff had a 2-day planning retreat to assess various aspects of the program.

As the staff discussed the pluses and minuses of the program, they discovered several things. Some staff stated that reports from field personnel indicated that many of the interns were struggling with classroom management. Other field personnel indicated that interns were not developing successful lesson plans. The purpose of readdressing curriculum in this instance would be to see if the particular area of concern (e.g., classroom management or lesson planning) had been fully and effectively developed in the curriculum, that all the standards are addressed appropriately and adequately.

The staff also had a discussion about the success of their interns on passing the state board exams that are aligned to state standards. Even though the program had a high passing rate over several years, they did find that scores were consistently lower in certain areas.

A discussion about the staff's own philosophies of standards-based curriculum was necessary. They felt the program at one time had looked at the alignment of their curriculum with the state standards, but at some point a drift away from standards had occurred. This had probably happened because of some of the reasons cited earlier in this chapter. Individual members had added elements to their curriculum based on the latest training they had attended, a passion they had about some aspect of the curriculum, or a variety of other reasons. This is called *standards drift*. As it occurred, teachers had unintentionally diminished their original focus and consequently drifted away from their alignment with the standards.

To help prepare for this project, in July 2003, the leadership of the Region XIII ECP attended the INTASC Academy, "Building Effective Standards-Based Teacher Preparation Assessment Systems," sponsored by the Council of Chief State School Officers, the American Association of Colleges for Teacher Education, and Alverno College. Included in the training was a process for performing a curriculum audit, to help a program learn exactly how closely it is aligned with standards, where it has gaps, and where there is overlap within a standard. As a result of attending the academy, the leaders of the Region XIII ECP began to consider using this audit process with their program curriculum.

The impetus for the audit was twofold. The first was to assure the current curriculum was appropriate. The state of Texas had adopted new standards for teachers who would be tested through new state board exams (the Texas Examination of Educator Standards, or TExES Framework). However, certain members of the Region XIII staff believed the current curriculum would be more than sufficient even with the new state standards because the program had a strong history of success in preparing participants for passing the previous exam. In fact, the passing rate of participants was always over 95%.

However, there was the second issue of interns not successfully implementing what they were taught in their training sessions. The feeling of the staff was that they had covered lesson planning and classroom environment early in preservice training and revisited it early during inservice training. They talked about how their interns' assignments for class during that part of their training were acceptable. However, there had to be a reason for this phenomenon—the success on assignments but the difficulty in demonstrating the skill in an actual classroom setting. And there had to be a solution.

The Region XIII staff then met together for the audit process they had learned at Alverno College. They placed long strips of butcher paper on the walls, one strip for each unit taught. The focus was on the TExES Pedagogy and Professional Responsibilities exam. Small slips of paper had been prepared with one TExES standard component, or indicator, on each slip of paper, color coded to indicate the staff member. Each staff member had a full set of TExES standards components. They were to take the slips of paper and place each standard under the course where they taught it. There was an envelope beside each strip of butcher paper for placing those standards not taught in any course (see Figure 4.1).

Figure 4.1   Working on the Audit Process

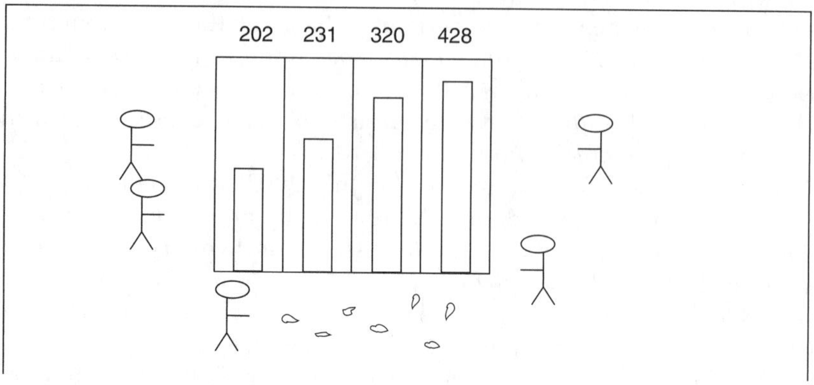

At the end of this exercise, the staff was very surprised. First, more indicators were in the envelopes than on the butcher paper. There were also many indicators showing up repetitively, demonstrating that many staff members were teaching the same indicators. Many indicators were placed for some courses; for others, few were placed. The next step, then, was for the staff to look at their findings, as shown on the butcher paper, and begin making decisions about the data.

To illustrate this part of the process further, examine Table 4.4. The Alverno Academy used this table to show the results of a curriculum audit of one university's education department. The numbers across the top of the table are college course numbers. The INTASC principles are listed down the first column. The knowledge, performance, and dispositions of each INTASC principle (indicated by k, p, or d) appear under each course where they are taught.

From this look at the university's curriculum, many questions arise. How can one course cover every single principle and all the indicators (course 385)? Why is course 390 even offered? Why do several courses cover performance indicator 5 (P5) in standard 4, but other indicators in this standard are only covered by one other course? Is there collaboration among the instructional staff as to who introduces the component, who develops the component, and who brings the component to mastery? Is there conversation in each class about prior knowledge of the component? Is the component ever assessed for mastery? Is it assessed in every class for mastery? The table also makes it clear that many of the INTASC indicators are not listed under any course. How do the students obtain understanding of the ones that are never covered?

Table 4.4 *Alpha Teacher Preparation Program*

Course → / Standard ↓	121	225	270	301	322	332	370	385	390	418	Psychology	Other
1 Content and Pedagogical Content	K3, 4 D1, 2, 3 P2, 5			K3, 4 D1, 2, 3 P2, 5	K3, 4 D4, 5 P1, 2, 5, 7	K3, 4 D1, 2, 3 P2, 5	All	All				
2 Human Development							All	All			K 1–3	
3 Diverse Learners		All	K all D2, 4 P1, 3, 7, 9				All	All				
4 Variety of Strategies and Higher Order Thinking	P5		P5	P5	P5	P5		All				
5 Learning Environment		K1–5 D1–4 P1–5						All				
6 Communication								All				Technology lab skills
7 Planning	K1–3			P4	P4		All	All				
8 Assessment						P1–6	All	All			K3	
9 Professional Development	K1, K2			K1, K2		K1, K2		All		K1, K2	K1, K2	
10 Relationships with Others			P2, P4					All		K1–3 P1–6		

Source: Council of Chief State School Officers, et al. (2003), INTASC Academy.

71

Other questions could be asked about the table, but it becomes very evident that much can be learned by any certification program through a curriculum audit, which can be a powerful tool for existing certification programs in moving to full alignment with state standards.

Region XIII's table looked similar to the one just discussed. The staff found many gaps as well as overlaps in their curriculum. They quickly determined that their curriculum was a big part of the problems discussed at their planning retreat.

Understanding the Concept of "Foundational"

Another important conversation by the staff was about the large amount of content available for them to teach. They were concerned about things that were not in the standards. They realized that in teacher education, there is a vast amount of knowledge that can be presented to potential teachers. Because the instructors of interns have been in the profession for a number of years, they have a wealth of knowledge about the discipline of teaching. They have developed this knowledge through experience, through attendance at many conferences, and through reading, study, and research.

In addition to this, new knowledge and emerging theories about the discipline continue to evolve and make their way to the forefront. There is never an end to what can be taught and learned by potential teachers. This is probably the biggest reason that certification programs have tended to develop their curriculum for breadth of knowledge rather than depth of knowledge. In their minds, there is simply too much to teach. So they teach a lot but have difficulty teaching anything very deeply.

One reason that standards and their components are so important is that they have been developed around what a *beginning* teacher should know and be able to do to be successful with students. Beginning teachers need basic core knowledge about teaching. However, they need this knowledge to a deep level of understanding so that when they enter the classroom, they have mastered that foundational knowledge. This depth of knowledge is the key to their ability to implement such knowledge about teaching skillfully in the classroom. When teachers comment that they did not learn in their preparation training what they needed to know about teaching, it often is not because it was not taught. It is because it was not understood at a depth that allowed it to be translated as skill in the classroom.

The Region XIII staff determined it is crucial to remember that the role of teacher education is to prepare *beginning* teachers. More knowledge and skill will evolve as the teacher gains experience and maturity in the teaching profession. It cannot and should not be assumed they will receive everything during the preservice training. Aligning curriculum to standards will help assure that only those basic concepts outlined in the standards are taught during preservice and will help prevent the tendency to want to include "everything I know."

It could easily be argued that new teachers need to enter the classroom fully prepared to impact student performance to the same extent that the experienced teacher does. Parents would certainly support this argument, as would many principals. In fact, the students in the new teacher's classroom deserve no less. However, *if* new teachers have a deep understanding of the core knowledge outlined in standards, they will have the skills to be successful with students their very first year. They will, of course, get better over time, but they won't be ineffective with their students during that first year. Also, the deeper an understanding they have of this core knowledge, the better they will be able to learn, understand, and assimilate new information about their craft as it is presented to them in continuing years.

How to Design Curriculum Around Standards

Use a Model

Now that program staff had familiarized themselves with standards, done an audit of the current curriculum, and given thought to the concept of necessary foundational knowledge, the next step was to actually put together the activities and assessments that would guide the delivery of their curriculum. Specifically, the staff began to ponder how they could take a number of standards, a lot of content, and shape it into engaging, thought-provoking, and meaningful learning. It was important to avoid an activity-based approach as well as a "covering the standards" approach. Most important was for the curriculum to impact learning *deliberately*. At this point for Region XIII ECP, *Understanding by Design* (UbD), by Wiggins and McTighe (1998), became the model that guided their curriculum development.

Many curriculum models are available, and many of them provide strong support for curriculum development efforts. Wiggins and McTighe even reference several of them in their book. Ultimately, the 'so-called magic' may not be in any particular model. Instead it is the disciplined use of a model that is good practice because the model provides a guideline that will assure consistency, as well as help bring about desired results.

Before sharing specific information about the Region XIII program curriculum, it will be important to have a basic understanding of the UbD model. The Region XIII ECP staff spent team meeting time studying and discussing the Wiggins and McTighe book to gain strong working knowledge of the model. Wiggins and McTighe first introduce this question, "How does one go about determining what is worth understanding amid a range of content standards and topics?" (p. 13). One guideline the researchers suggest is to think about what is important for the program's interns to remember 40 years from now. If it is that important, it is a "big idea" and worth taking to a deep level of understanding. They then offer four filters for selecting ideas to teach for what they call Enduring Understandings:

1. To what extent does the idea, topic, or process represent a "big idea" having enduring value beyond the classroom?
2. To what extent does the idea, topic, or process reside at the heart of the discipline?
3. To what extent does the idea, topic, or process require uncoverage?
4. To what extent does the idea, topic, or process offer potential for engaging students? (p. 23)

Under these Enduring Understandings, standards can be clustered.

Cluster Standards

If a teacher of teachers was to attempt to check off each indicator within any given framework of standards, what would probably happen would be a disjointed presentation of *factlets* (small pieces of information) to the students. Simply presenting individual indicators does not make for good teaching. For example, in a history class, a teacher could require the students to know the names of an area's rivers, the names of the area's present and past leaders, the names of the wars in which it has been involved, and so on. These are all factlets of information. However, none of this gives the student a deep understanding of the history of the area.

Instead, it is important to look at the indicators and find "big ideas" among clusters. For example, using the previously discussed framework by Danielson, there are four domains with several components and indicators under each domain. Using Table 4.5 to look specifically at Domain 2: The Classroom Environment, there are 5 components with 15 indicators. A teacher could cover each indicator separately, and the student's learning and comprehension of such a disjointed set of factlets would be far less than ideal. Under component 2d, for example, the intern could be given factlets about different structures used for monitoring student misbehavior, such as proximity, acknowledging appropriate behavior, a 3:1 ratio of positive to negative interactions, and so on. Simply receiving (and perhaps memorizing) factlets does not translate into demonstrated skill in the classroom. Interns try implementing their toolbox of tricks (the factlets) and when their toolbox is empty, they struggle with what to try next. This is because the students have not developed a deep understanding of the content. But if the teacher looked for big ideas within this domain, the entire domain could be taught to a depth of understanding that would much more easily be translated into practice in the classroom.

Another step in the *Understanding by Design* model is to develop Essential Questions for each unit that align with the Enduring Understandings. These

Table 4.5   The Classroom Environment

Domain 2: The Classroom Environment

- Component 2a: Creating an Environment of Respect and Rapport
  - Teacher interaction with students
  - Student interaction
- Component 2b: Establishing a Culture for Learning
  - Importance of the content
  - Student pride in work
  - Expectations for learning and achievement
- Component 2c: Managing Classroom Procedures
  - Management of instructional groups
  - Management of transitions
  - Management of materials and supplies
  - Performance of noninstructional duties
  - Supervision of volunteers and paraprofessionals
- Component 2d: Managing Student Behavior
  - Expectations
  - Monitoring of student behavior
  - Response to student misbehavior
- Component 2e: Organizing Physical Space
  - Safety and arrangement of furniture
  - Accessibility to learning and use of physical resources

Source: Danielson, C. (2007). *Enhancing Professional Practice: A Framework for Teaching,* Second Edition. Alexandria, VA: Association for Supervision and Curriculum Development.

Essential Questions can be used in many ways to help guide the intern to a deeper level of understanding of the standards. Essential Questions should stimulate thought and/or discussion and spark more questions. They are not answerable with finality. They push to the heart or essence of the content (Wiggins & McTighe, 1998, pp. 29–30). Some Enduring Understandings and Essential Questions are illustrated later in the chapter. The Wiggins and McTighe "backward by design" process would have the teacher develop specific Enduring Understandings and Essential Questions that would then guide the development of the assessment as well as the learning activities for each unit or lesson.

Teach for Understanding

Once the Enduring Understandings have been developed for the course, the next step is determining what will be used to assess the understanding of these concepts. The several types of assessments are discussed elsewhere in this book.

For teachers, performance-based assessments are useful to determine whether or not teachers can actually put into practice the knowledge they have learned. Ongoing informal assessments as well as other types of assessments are also important. Once the alignment of the assessments to the Enduring Understanding has been finalized, a determination about what evidence will be accepted to assure teacher understanding must occur. This would mean developing a rubric or some other tool for determining acceptable evidence. Finally, learning activities for teacher-candidates would be planned to assure success on the assessment and bring about the deep understanding of the concept. This is the backward by design process outlined in *Understanding by Design*. It is the opposite of what is usually done when planning curriculum. Frequently teachers first develop their learning activities, then determine how they will assess the knowledge gained from those activities, and finally consider what the acceptable evidence might look like (see Figure 4.2).

Figure 4.2   Typical Planning Process

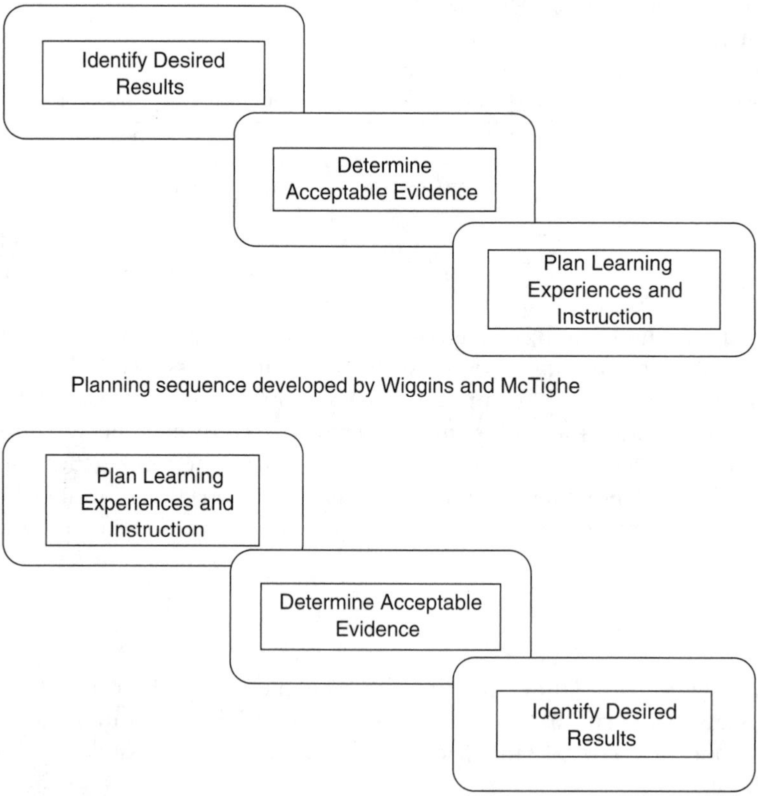

Identify Desired Results

Determine Acceptable Evidence

Plan Learning Experiences and Instruction

Planning sequence developed by Wiggins and McTighe

Plan Learning Experiences and Instruction

Determine Acceptable Evidence

Identify Desired Results

By first determining the Enduring Understandings desired in the lesson or unit, and then determining how to assess whether students have acquired a deep understanding about them, the teacher is much more assured that students will take away the knowledge and skills desired from the unit. This process works equally well whether teacher candidates are the students or the teacher-candidates are the teachers. It is a process they can and should use in developing their own curriculum units.

Obviously the process is much more complex than just described. Only a simple overview has been provided here, but it should give you a sense of what is involved. When curriculum has been developed in this way, the instructor of interns is teaching for depth of knowledge rather than just breadth of knowledge. The instructor is no longer thinking about "checking off the standards" but instead is focusing on that deep level of knowledge about the Enduring Understanding that covers the cluster of indicators rather than each one as a separate end in itself.

Use Enduring Understandings

The Region XIII ECP spent many weeks simply studying the *Understanding by Design* book to obtain a clear and complete understanding of the model. Staff worked in teams to develop the new curriculum based on the model, but eventually one staff member was asked to complete the work to assure the consistency to the model and the desired level of rigor of the courses. The results produced a strong curriculum that greatly increased the performance of the Region XIII ECP interns in the classroom during their internship year as well as success on the state board exams.

To give an example of how the model worked, look at Danielson's Standard 2 Classroom Environment shown in Table 4.5. Region XIII staff used the following prompt to help them determine their Enduring Understandings: "When a master teacher has a *deep understanding* of these indicators, what do they inherently know and do?" Based on this thought process, the Enduring Understandings developed by Region XIII ECP curriculum specialists for this standard were the following:

1. Behavior is communication.
2. Behavior is a content area.
3. The teacher is the decisive element.

The team felt these statements met the criteria of Enduring Understandings identified earlier. They represented a big idea having value beyond the classroom. They were at the heart of the discipline. They definitely required uncoverage. They had great potential for engaging students.

From these Enduring Understandings, all the components and indicators from this standard can be explored. As they are explored, a depth of under-standing begins to evolve that will enable the interns to implement each indicator in the classroom. For example, interns will know they need to have rules and consequences posted (a factlet), but with the deeper level of understanding they now know the "why" behind that procedure: so teachers can refer to them when they are teaching behavior and they can refer back to them when they need to reteach a behavioral lesson. They are visual reminders to students of the expectations. But with a deep knowledge around the Enduring Understandings, interns can no longer make excuses for why behavior is occurring or for their inability to control the behavior. Now they understand that they are the decisive element and there are no excuses. To once again go back to a previous criterion, these are things that master teachers inherently know and do.

Use Essential Questions

The staff also spent much time developing Essential Questions to guide and enhance instruction. The first box in Figure 4.3 shows an example of a typical objective from Domain 1: Designing Instruction. Think about the different types of discussions that might occur if a teacher was developing a lesson around the objective statement in the first box. However, using the Essential Questions in the second box, the interns are quickly drawn into discussions with each other about their understanding behind the questions.

Figure 4.3   Using Essential Questions to Bring Depth of Understanding

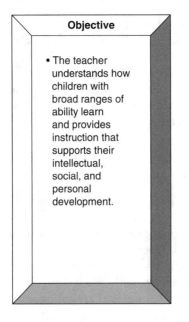

Objective

• The teacher understands how children with broad ranges of ability learn and provides instruction that supports their intellectual, social, and personal development.

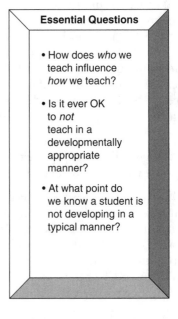

Essential Questions

• How does *who* we teach influence *how* we teach?

• Is it ever OK to *not* teach in a developmentally appropriate manner?

• At what point do we know a student is not developing in a typical manner?

For Region XIII ECP, these Essential Questions are woven through the learning activities. They are used as a sponge activity to start conversations when the interns enter the classroom. They are brought back into class and/or small-group discussions as the lesson activities occur. They are used to wrap up a unit as a check for understanding. Continually throughout the lesson, over several days, the interns come back to these questions. The answers evolve for them over this time period as they gain deeper understanding of the concept. By the time the lesson is assessed, they are very clear about why the developmental level of a student is important. They are clear about how this is important for planning, for behavior management, and for instructional expectations in the classroom. Rather than memorizing the names of theorists about child development and what the theorists espouse, interns now know why these theories are important and how to implement the theories in their practice.

To give an example of the merits of this type of curriculum development, using Enduring Understandings and Essential Questions, think about a first-year teacher early in the year. The program supervisor goes in to observe and finds the typical issues with classroom management. If the intern had been taught using the method of "checking off standards" or of teaching factlets, the program supervisor might approach the classroom management problem something like this:

Program supervisor: You were having a lot of problems with behavior. Did you enforce your five classroom rules that are posted?

Intern: I try, but it doesn't seem to work. They ignore the rules.

Program supervisor: Well, did you follow the consequences that you have posted?

Intern: I try, but sometimes I'm to the last consequence in the sequence by 10 o'clock.

Program supervisor: Have you called parents?

Intern: Yes, but they don't seem to care or at least don't do anything about it.

This conversation could continue for several minutes with the teacher always having a reason why the factlets of knowledge she was given in her training were not working. In fact, she is continually shifting the blame to some outside source or issue.

But let's look at the conversation when the intern has been taught using the curriculum designed with the *Understanding by Design* model, using Enduring Understandings and Essential Questions.

Program supervisor: You were having a lot of problems with behavior. We know behavior is communication. What do you think the behavior was telling you today?

Intern: Well, maybe I didn't have a good pace to my lesson and they were frustrated. However, I know Ethan was very

	upset when he came in this morning, and sometimes when he's that way, he can set off the whole class.
Program supervisor:	Because we also know that behavior is a content area, what behavioral lessons have you taught that have addressed these issues?
Intern:	Actually, I haven't done a behavioral lesson in several weeks. That would probably be a good thing to do tomorrow. I know I'm the decisive element in this class and that it's up to me to make good decisions about my students. Some of my decisions today weren't good, but I will have a plan for that tomorrow.

When the intern has knowledge of just the three Enduring Understandings delineated earlier, the conversation is not about a lot of so-called tricks that might be used to improve the classroom environment. The conversation moves to a different level of understanding.

In essence, the staff found that this process brought about a curriculum that provided meaningful, deep, provocative inquiry into the content. The curriculum led to interns learning how to use the content. Conversely, the previous curriculum brought lack of understanding, which led to amnesia, misunderstanding, and rigid knowledge. Rigid knowledge can be illustrated using the same scenario as just described. The intern might have been taught behavior management strategies, such as using proximity, positive reinforcement, or perhaps behavior contracts. With rigid knowledge, if the classroom situation is not the same or similar to the training scenario, the intern does not know how to generalize the information to new situations. Deep understanding brings about the ability to generalize the knowledge.

The importance of curriculum, its alignment to standards, its development based on a model, and the significance of consistency of instruction is clear. Curriculum must not be a hodgepodge of information, thrown together at the last minute, or even planned over time with no thought as to where it is leading or what it is following. Curriculum should be well crafted and well timed; it should be relevant and engaging. From the beginning, there should be an end in mind, a purpose. That purpose must be none other than the success of the teacher with the students in the classroom.

Even in the pilot year of using the new curriculum, the staff of the Region XIII ECP saw tremendous differences in the depth of knowledge of their interns. Their classroom practices with their students clearly reflected what they had learned. ECP staff would see great bulletin boards in classrooms that listed math and science Enduring Understandings as the interns internalized this way of designing lessons. The discussions during field visits were at a much deeper level. The persistence of effort had a big payoff. The program moved from using what feels important to teach, to using standards to determine what to teach; from using activities to guide instruction to using assessment objectives to target instruction.

Curriculum Delivery System

As stated earlier, the curriculum delivery system used in imparting the curriculum to the student requires thoughtful consideration. The Region XIII program has full-time staff members who deliver all instruction in a cohort model. They keep the same group of interns from the beginning of the program to the end, which enables the program to have all staff trained in the delivery of the program's curriculum and also to monitor its delivery.

The Region XIII ECP has made a commitment to modeling best practice in their delivery of instruction. Many instructional practices are taught covertly by using them in the delivery of the curriculum. A common thread that runs through all the trainings is the expectation to model an instructional delivery strategy, such as group discussion or cooperative learning, or a strategy, such as developing graphic organizers, and then ask these questions:

- What instructional strategy did we use for this concept?
- Why do you think that strategy was chosen for this concept?
- What are other situations when this instructional strategy could be used?
- What other instructional strategies might also have been appropriately used?

This approach gives the Region XIII ECP interns an opportunity to see different instructional strategies and also helps them to learn what guides the decision about which strategy to use when the intern is the classroom teacher.

Online Instruction

Many educational entities are migrating to an online delivery of instruction. This modality of instruction has many merits. Besides allowing participants to attend class without driving a long distance to the university or program location, it also allows flexibility. However, the Region XIII staff felt that many concepts in the preparation of teaching are best learned through modeling and practicing.

For example, how to set up guided reading centers or how to teach math concepts with manipulatives might best be learned as hands-on activities. If so, the best online instruction for these types of pedagogy concepts would be video streaming or other methods for demonstrating the concept. Moving interns to a deep level of understanding sometimes requires dialogue or discourse. To enable interns to have this opportunity, the use of student discussion or practice through a conference board, chat room, or other method can provide a way for participants to engage in dialogue about the concepts they are learning. The Region XIII staff was very thoughtful in determining how each part of the curriculum should be delivered and ultimately chose a blended model of both online and face-to-face methods. The content of each part of the curriculum drove the decision of which method to use.

Contracted Presenters

Many educational entities, particularly those that are not university based, use contracted consultants to deliver their curriculum. This presents some unique challenges for assuring the content of their presentations is standards based.

Region XIII staff had found that the contracted consultants were often not interested in developing new curriculum aligned to standards or using standards-aligned curriculum that was already developed. In Region XIII ECP's experience, many contracted consultants have their own content, which they frequently use and are not interested in changing to align to standards.

Additionally, a contracted consultant is often accustomed to presenting to seasoned teachers. Consequently, the contracted consultant may not understand the concept discussed earlier of assuring that the curriculum is foundational. At times when Region XIII staff did choose to use contracted consultants, they tried to overcome these challenges and make certain the curriculum was aligned and appropriate by clearly specifying in the contract what was expected and then monitoring its delivery.

Role of the Program Administrator

After spending many months studying and then developing new curriculum, Region XIII staff decided it would also be important to think about what happens once the standards have been set, the curriculum aligned with the standards, and the program delivery format decided. What happens next? It became clear that the next steps are within the domain of the program administrator. The curriculum itself is a fluid document. The program administrator has a large role in directing and guiding those dynamics.

Determine the Appropriateness of the Current Curriculum

The program administrator is most frequently the leader who either initially establishes the curriculum or determines if a curriculum redesign project is needed. The program administrator is in a position to facilitate the process of design or redesign and to assure it is completed correctly. These responsibilities may require significant determination and perseverance.

For example, when the Region XIII ECP staff began the process to align their curriculum with standards, the program administrator's estimation and expectation was a 12- to 18-month process. Four years later, after much hard work, many opportunities to give up and return to the former curriculum, and many restarts, the staff finally finished the curriculum, although *finished* is in itself a relative word. Without the perseverance of the program administrator, the Region XIII curriculum development and alignment initiative would have been another one of those initiatives to have fallen by the wayside.

Guard the Curriculum

It is easy for any staff person to want to add to or change the curriculum. The program administrator is the one person who is in the position to make decisions about those changes. An approval process is needed to determine the appropriateness of changes, additions, and deletions. It is the program administrator's role to see that this process is used and not bypassed. Without such a process in place, the standards drift discussed earlier is almost certain to occur.

At the Region XIII ECP, before the process was even fully completed, staff members were asking about adding a module about one thing or a video about another. The process in place for making decisions about these requests involves a series of questions to determine if changes should be permitted:

- Why is the addition/deletion/change necessary?
- What will the addition bring to the curriculum that is not already there or that is better than what is there?
- If it is a deletion, how will students understand the concept after this deletion?
- How does the addition align to the Enduring Understandings for the standard?
- How will the addition be assessed?

Up to this point, this process has continued to ensure that the program's curriculum remains aligned to the standards and that the rigor remains the high level brought about through the *Understanding by Design* model.

Another important role in guarding the curriculum is to make certain a plan is in place for orienting new staff to the curriculum. At Region XIII, current staff members are designated to mentor new staff. One of the responsibilities of that role is orientation to the curriculum. Having a developed curriculum in place greatly assists new staff because they can bring consistency to the delivery of the curriculum almost immediately. However, someone has to make sure the new staff has been trained not only in how to use the curriculum, but also has an understanding of the model used in developing the curriculum. At the Region XIII ECP, this means that new staff must understand the concepts around *Understanding by Design* and also understand the developed curriculum.

Facilitate Ongoing Assessment of the Curriculum

Every staff meeting at Region XIII ECP involves time for discussion about the curriculum. Data are collected to substantiate whether or not the curriculum is successful in preparing teachers. Decisions are made based on analysis of the data.

Through these discussions and data analysis, the program administrator can get a sense of the level of understanding of each staff member around the curriculum. These discussions help the program administrator determine whether or not the curriculum is being presented appropriately and effectively. This information leads to greater and more germane input for staff evaluations, personal professional development plans, and contract renewals.

Staff meetings also give the program administrator an opportunity to share changes that occur at the state level with regard to the standards. When such changes are made, the curriculum must once again be reviewed or audited to be sure these changes are embedded. Without this vigilant monitoring, new gaps or redundancies may occur.

Even within an aligned curriculum, new research can become available that will change some of the content of the curriculum. This information is discussed at team meetings with decisions made there regarding how it will be incorporated without developing standards drift. The decision could be that the new information is not a part of the state standards and should be left for district-provided staff development. Or the decision could be that the new information should be incorporated into the program's curriculum. Either way, it is an intentional decision, using procedures developed specifically for that purpose.

Observe the Delivery of the Curriculum and Hold Staff Accountable

In education there has been a habit or practice of "shutting our doors and doing what we want to do." Because of the ever-growing expectation and demands for accountability surrounding student success, this practice is fading in the public schools. It needs to go away in teacher education also. In the end, this will only occur when the program administrator is fully aware of whether or not each staff member or contracted consultant is presenting the approved curriculum, and whether or not he or she is doing it with the expected level of competence.

Just as campus principals have a responsibility to do periodic walk-throughs in each teacher's classroom, the program administrator will learn much from spending time in the training sessions provided by the program. But sometimes the program is not set up in a way that makes this feasible. Even without time in these sessions, assessment data can be used to see if there is consistent intern success across program staff or program courses that might indicate lack of appropriate delivery of the curriculum.

Provide Professional Development Initiatives for Program Staff

All staff benefit from having a personal professional development plan. Each Region XIII staff member submits a plan to the program administrator annually. Instructors need to be on the cutting edge of the research and best practices in education. The graduates of any teacher preparation program should leave with the latest knowledge available.

To achieve this, three areas are included in all professional development plans for Region XIII instructors:

1. Ongoing training in the use of the designed curriculum and the model on which it is based
2. Opportunities for learning the latest research and best practices
3. Opportunities for learning and enhancing instructional practices to improve delivery of the curriculum

Use Curriculum Assessments to Determine Status of Participants

If the curriculum and its delivery are successful in preparing effective teachers, then the assessments on which that curriculum is based will give credible information about the ability of the program participants to be effective in a classroom of students. At Region XIII these assessments are part of the big picture that is examined when determining whether or not a participant will be allowed to move to the internship or student teaching phase of the program and whether or not the participant will receive a recommendation for the teacher certificate. This information is also used to drive discussions at planning meetings about next steps for the program in supporting the interns.

Assure Passage of the Flame

At some point, every program administrator leaves the program. At Region XIII, the program administrator left the program just as the process was being completed. This could have been catastrophic if the curriculum development process had been administrator driven. It was vital that the curriculum project not fall apart when she left. To avoid this, the program administrator should develop and implement a plan to assure the sustainability of the program and the curriculum that has made it successful. The Region XIII administrator had staff available who had been with the process from the beginning and had a big investment in it. But in interviewing for the new administrator, many questions were asked about prospective candidates' understanding of curriculum design, about the Wiggins and McTighe model, and about their understanding of standards. It was important to select a new administrator who would continue to support the project.

Sometimes staff can be so strong in their beliefs of the merits and worth of the curriculum that they are the ones who lead it forward and assure it is sustained. Sometimes the program administrator arranges for a time of transition or overlapping employment with the new program administrator so training can occur. A sharing of the history of the program and its curriculum alignment process is an important part of that training.

Conclusion

Douglas Reeves (2002) makes an important observation about standards when he says, "If standards are to be successfully implemented, then many of the traditional ways of doing things must cease" (p. 9). He is addressing this issue in a K–12 setting, but it is true for teacher preparation also. Some examples of practices he says must cease to be acceptable are the following:

- Attendance (or seat time) is sufficient to gain credit.
- A "D" is a passing grade.
- A great program is measured by the quantity and creativity of its elective offerings.
- Academic core curriculum classes are identical in structure and length for every student. (pp. 10–11)

For a teacher preparation program, these might also include the following:

- A great program is measured by the number of teachers it certifies.
- Academic core classes are deemed successful based solely on passage rates of students.

When the Region XIII program began its study of standards and its curriculum alignment initiative, the goal was to guarantee that interns had the best training possible so they would be successful with the students in their classrooms. That focus guided every decision. Their belief was that their program and in essence all certification programs must begin to measure success by how proficient their interns are when they enter the school classroom. Are their students making appropriate academic progress? To assure this, certification programs must provide their interns with the best instruction possible so they have the understandings they need to employ the skills that will bring about student success. There is not time to wait 3 or 4 years while they develop their teaching acumen. Principals who will be hiring these interns need to be confident that the interns will be effective educators for the students in their classrooms. The heightened accountability now in place in all states makes this more important than ever to principals, superintendents, school boards, and communities.

The job of the teacher certification program is not simply to make certain their graduates have the educational credential. Instead, it is to know for certain that the teachers have the knowledge and skill to educate others effectively. The task of certification programs is not to put a body where before there has not been a body. The task is not to provide a forum so that potential teachers can jump through the necessary hoops for obtaining a certification. The task is not simply to assure they meet the qualification of "highly qualified teacher" established in the No Child Left Behind legislation. The task is to be sure there are *high-quality* teachers in every classroom, every day, beginning with their first day in the classroom. Strong well-designed curriculum is one of the best means for accomplishing this task. It may be the only predictable and sustainable means for accomplishing this lofty and worthwhile goal.

References

Council of Chief State School Officers, National Council for Accreditation of Teacher Education, Alverno College. (2003). *INTASC Academy: Building effective standards-based teacher preparation assessment systems.*

Danielson, C. (1996). *Enhancing professional practice: A framework for teaching.* Alexandria, VA: Association for Supervision and Curriculum Development.

Humphrey, D. C., Wechsler, M. E., & Hough, H. J. (2005). *Characteristics of effective alternative teacher certification programs.* Menlo Park, CA: SRI International.

Interstate New Teacher Assessment and Support Consortium (INTASC). (1992). *Model standards for beginning teacher licensing, assessment and development: A resource for state dialogue.* Washington, DC: Author.

Marzano, R. (2003). *What works in schools.* Alexandria, VA: Association for Supervision and Curriculum Development.

Reeves, D. B. (2002). *Making standards work.* Denver: Center for Performance Assessment.

U.S. Department of Health and Human Services. (2004). *Alternative routes to teacher certification.* Washington, DC: Author.

Wiggins, G., & McTighe, J. (1998). *Understanding by design.* Alexandria, VA: Association for Supervision and Curriculum Development.

5

Candidate Assessment

Eileen McDaniel and Karen Wilde
Florida

"If you don't know where you're going, any place will do."
Alice in Wonderland

*I*nvesting the energy and resources needed to create an alternative teacher certification program will not lead to the goal of successful student learning without the guidance of a map. A solid candidate assessment system is the map that defines each program's destination. When driven by established standards for both teachers and students, the candidate assessment system signals the direction for curriculum content and produces the documentation that each program candidate has demonstrated essential teaching competencies. Whereas the creative hallmark of alternative certification programs is the offering of teacher training curriculum through nontraditional paths, a multitude of delivery options does not by itself meet the litmus test for an effective program. If there is no coherent system of standards-based documentation that each prospective teacher can, in fact, facilitate successful student achievement, we can only ask, "So what?" This chapter provides a guide to ensure that your alternative certification program can respond with confidence to the question of, "So what?" via systematic evidence of each candidate's success as an effective teacher.

Standards-Based Assessment

Standards, in the context of educator preparation programs, are the most important tool in planning an assessment system. They give a clear picture of what teachers will be expected to do to meet requirements for high quality or "competence" that will lead to state licensure. They also form the basis for the curriculum that is the foundation of the professional development training program of educators.

Common Core of Teacher Knowledge

A standards-based assessment system for educator preparation programs, including alternative certification programs, must be constructed on the premise that common core of teacher knowledge exists. This core forms the foundation to ensure that every teacher in every classroom has met teaching standards aligned with student learning standards. A quality standards-based assessment system provides the tools to assess teachers in consistent ways and to obtain evidence of validity, reliability, and fairness.

Aligned with State and National Standards

Alternative certification programs that prepare teachers who possess noneducation degrees and thus have not participated in a traditional teacher preparation program must be able to demonstrate the knowledge and skills set forth in national and state standards, including accreditation agencies such as the National Council of Teacher Education (NCATE) and specialty professional associations in the subject content areas. Possessing an understanding of these standards will assist in designing an assessment system that can objectively identify areas that teachers need to improve their performance (i.e., measuring teacher competence).

A standards-based assessment system must begin with this question: "What does an effective teacher need to know and be able to do?" A close examination of the standards that form the basis of teacher education should yield a follow-up question: "How do we know that the teacher has acquired the knowledge and skills specified in the standards at some minimal level of competence?" This means that the individual elements of the standards must be operationally defined in terms of job-related measures of the teacher's performance, whether it is a written product or something performed in the classroom. In both instances, the job-related performance "task" can be designed to provide data on teacher competence defined by recognized standards of the teaching profession and can be scored objectively.

As an illustrative example, Florida developed and adopted a set of 12 competencies or practices—termed the Florida Educator Accomplished Practices (FEAPs)—that specify what teachers are expected to know and be able to do. The adoption of these teacher competencies was part of the national transition to standards-based education, that is, the use of an interrelated set of standards that outline what students should know and be able to do, and performance tasks that require students to demonstrate what they have learned. FEAPs draw from a set of principles developed by the Council of Chief State School Officers (CCSSO)—the Interstate New Teacher Assessment and Support Consortium (INTASC)—that define what all teachers, nationwide, should know, be able to do, and value. The competencies established in the FEAP are for teachers what Florida's "Sunshine State Standards" are for students. Just as K–12 schools must ensure that students have learned and demonstrated the established student standards, educator preparation programs, including alternative certification routes, must ensure that teachers have demonstrated all of the FEAPs (the essential skills and general knowledge needed to teach), as well as the subject area content knowledge required to support Florida's Sunshine State Standards.

The FEAPs cover such recognizable topics as "Assessment," "Planning," "Communication," "Knowledge of Subject Matter," "Learning Environment," and "Technology." Expectations, or benchmarks, are provided with brief descriptions for each practice at three levels of experience:

- "Preprofessional," or what Florida expects teachers who have just completed their teaching degree to know and be able to do
- "Professional," for those teachers who have met requirements for Florida's 5-year renewable Professional Educator Certificate
- "Accomplished," for those teachers who have demonstrated outstanding performance

Participants in Florida's alternative certification programs are required to demonstrate each practice at the "Preprofessional" level.

For example, in the FEAP entitled "Assessment," this is preprofessional descriptor for the practice: "The preprofessional teacher collects and uses data gathered from a variety of sources. These sources include both traditional and alternate assessment strategies. Furthermore, the teacher can identify and match the students' instructional plans with their cognitive, social, linguistic, cultural, emotional, and physical needs." You will note "student outcomes" are an integral part of the practice.

Each of the FEAPs also has a set of sample key indicators that are all linked to job-related skills and behaviors. In the preceding example, "Assessment," 13 sample key indicators are outlined at the "Preprofessional" level that will assist in determining satisfactory demonstration of the practice. Examples of sample key indicators for "Assessment" include the following:

- Employs traditional and alternative assessment strategies in determining students' mastery of specified outcomes
- Modifies instruction based on assessed student performance
- Maintains observational and anecdotal records to monitor students' development

Not all indicators are required to be demonstrated for satisfactory performance. More importantly, a variety of indicators must be successfully and consistently demonstrated over time.

Driven by Student Outcomes

The concept of job-related performance cannot be underestimated. To assess the performance of a teacher, it must be done in the context of the classroom in which he or she teaches. If a standard requires that a teacher be able to manage a classroom, it will be important for the assessor to *see* this standard performed—both in the production of a written classroom management plan and the actual act of observing the teacher working with students in the classroom. Moreover, in developing job-related performance tasks, we must remember that all assessment should be performed in the context of the outcome of our instruction—student learning growth.

When developing Florida's assessment system for use by school districts in their state-approved district alternative certification programs, Florida ensured that its assessment system covered the intent, depth, and breadth of each practice by developing a total of 41 assessment tasks correlated to the indicators of each FEAP and to the national standards from INTASC. Each of the assessment tasks is designed to provide information to an assessor and/or support team on how well the teacher is learning and implementing the FEAP. Two types of assessment tasks are included within the assessment system: product assessments (e.g., lesson plans, resource file) and performance assessments (e.g., live performance in the classroom is observed). In addition, the assessment tasks were carefully crafted to ensure that the teacher can demonstrate his or her competence in all of the critical aspects of each of the FEAP.

One of the assessment tasks that is a part of Florida's Assessment System for Alternative Certification Programs for the FEAP "Assessment" is entitled *Classroom Assessment System;* it is a "product" task whereby the program candidate must present concrete evidence of his or her competency in this area. This task is aligned to four different FEAP indicators and six INTASC indicators and includes the following description: "The teacher develops a classroom assessment system for one grading period. The product includes lists of outcomes, pre-assessment activities, and traditional and alternative assessment strategies, as well as a copy of the teacher's assessment recordkeeping system or gradebook." Four additional tasks, targeting seven additional FEAP indicators, are included in the Assessment System that targets the demonstration of the FEAP "Assessment." As a result, the teacher is required consistently to demonstrate, with depth and breadth, key essential skills and behaviors that ultimately impact student outcomes and performance.

Basic Ingredients of Sound Assessment

Now that we have set the stage for a standards-based assessment system for program candidates, we need to ensure that our assessments are sound. A sound standards-based assessment system for providers of alternative certification needs to have assessment practices that are fair and will yield evaluative information about teacher performance that is accurate and consistent. With accurate information that is collected consistently and free of bias, decision makers who determine if an individual is a competent teacher can be confident about their diagnoses of teacher performance. The basic ingredients that support confident decision making regarding a teacher's competency are validity, reliability, and fairness.

Validity

Validity is the most important property for program developers to consider as they develop a sound assessment system. Validity concerns the extent to which interpretations of assessment results will be appropriate, meaningful, and useful (Gronlund, 1993). Questions you might ask include, "Do the scoring instruments measure what they are supposed to measure? Are they providing the right kind of evidence for decisions about teacher quality? For standards-based assessments, are the criteria being measured truly reflective of the intent of the standard?"

To ensure that the results of the assessment system are valid, assessment developers can draw on various forms of evidence. Because we cannot measure every aspect of what a standard represents, an assessment system typically measures only a sample of the tasks teachers can perform within the standard the teacher is being assessed. For example, Florida's Educator Accomplished Practice on "Assessment" has 14 sample key indicators of performance that could be measured to determine competency in this area. The state's assessment system has carefully selected 11 of these indicators as a representative sample of what teachers should know and be able to do to infer competence in this standard. Therefore, in constructing a sound assessment system, key teacher outcomes from the standards must be identified that will represent what teachers should know and do, and measures must be created that target specific performances or behaviors that can be demonstrated by the teacher.

Studying the content of an assessment system to confirm its validity is a critical step in the development of a legally solid system. A validity study looks for representativeness, relevance, proportionality, and job relatedness of the assessment system across all standards, and it adjusts the system if needed. Florida's assessment system has been studied to confirm its validity (*Analysis of District Coordinators' Validity Questionnaire of Assessment Tasks*, Florida Department of Education, February 2004). Alternative certification program coordinators reviewed and rated each of the system's 41 assessment tasks according to *frequency* (How frequently should the skills and knowledge being measured be evidenced by good teachers?), *criticality* (How important is each skill being measured?), and *authenticity* (Do the tasks really measure what teachers do?). The analysis of the coordinators' responses confirmed that the assessment tasks are representative of what effective teachers do, relevant to effective teaching, and job related. Furthermore, the validity study ensured that the tasks are representative of the knowledge and skills that Florida teachers need to demonstrate their mastery of Florida's Educator Accomplished Practices.

Reliability

Another essential ingredient of a sound standards-based assessment system is the reliability of the assessment instruments. Reliability concerns the degree to which the assessment tasks are free from measurement errors. Any assessment task is just an estimate of the level of teacher performance. Errors can occur for a number of reasons, including variations in assessment conditions and inconsistency of scoring. Questions that may be asked in deciding if an assessment system is reliable might include "Would the decisions made on using the scoring instruments be consistent over time and across raters (different assessors or evaluators)? Are the results dependable?" A reliable assessment system, then, gives a consistent picture of teacher performance over time and between one type of measurement or another. A teacher who has mastered a particular skill should be able consistently to perform well on multiple measures to assess performance. Therefore, when multiple means of assessment are used to determine what teachers know and can do, they increase the level of reliability in which assessors can make sound assessment decisions.

To address the property of reliability, Florida's assessment system contains multiple measurement opportunities that require the teacher to demonstrate each of the standards in a variety of ways. A teacher candidate who successfully completes the entire assessment system has demonstrated consistently over time the key measures of all the standards and in different venues. Florida has also developed an online Assessor Training tool that includes practice activities for objectively scoring rubrics for assessment tasks. As a result of this training, assessors are better prepared to score the assessment task products consistently and thus improve the interrater reliability between scorers.

Fairness

The final basic ingredient of a sound assessment system is fairness. A fair assessment system includes several key features. First, alternative certification program candidates must be made aware of what is expected: what behaviors will be assessed, how will it be determined whether or not a skill has been demonstrated adequately, what are the scoring criteria for an overall decision of competent teaching performance? Candidates also need to have opportunities for feedback and improvement prior to a final decision regarding overall teaching competence. Finally, all aspects of the assessment system must be free of bias that could have the effect of discriminating against any legally protected population, such as race or gender (Wilkerson & Lang, 2003).

Maintaining a data bank of all candidates' assessment ratings, cross-checked against demographic information about the candidates, can help detect possible biases in the assessment system. By comparing candidates' performance ratings across individual assessment tasks with candidate demographics, program managers can determine whether or not any candidate group appears to be having more difficulty on a particular assessment item than the rest of the candidates. The biased item or items can then be corrected to ensure fairness to all candidates.

Fostering Objectivity Through Scoring Rubrics

We have now established the foundation of a topographical assessment map by identifying the common core of teacher knowledge we want our program candidates to demonstrate. We have then proceeded to the next layer by defining each teaching skill operationally into sets of job-related performance tasks that assessors will observe in the context of student learning growth. We have also ensured that our system includes the basic elements of validity, reliability, and fairness. What, then, is the next layer of our assessment map?

In good teaching practice, the learner must know precisely what outcome is expected. It is equally essential for the alternative certification program and its assessment system to demonstrate principles of effective teaching practice. Therefore, how can program developers do an even better job of leading the way to the destination of effective teaching? If candidates can see the common core of teacher knowledge, what more do they need to know as they aim for their target of successful program completion? And what else do assessors need to know as they determine who the successful candidates are? They need more explicit directions on the assessment map, a series of easy-to-see road signs or markers that guide the developing teacher, along with the assessor, to the final destination of successful program completion via competent teaching performance. The set of road markers are rubrics.

Clarify Expectations

As road signs that help lead the way along our assessment map, a set of rubrics for each performance task clarifies the following expectations while exemplifying good teaching practices by:

- Stating the level of knowledge that is expected.
- Establishing the dimensions of quality that are expected.
- Describing the levels of achievement that can be performed (e.g., the minimal level that will be accepted, as well as clear descriptions of what higher levels of quality may look like).
- Defining explicit criteria for rating each achievement level.

- Outlining the scale that pinpoints where the cumulative ratings place the teacher's performance on the continuum of quality that is expected. (Slatterly, 2006)

Provide Objective Rules

Objectivity by assessors is essential in evaluating a candidate's performance. Scoring rubrics provide objective rules that further define observable and measurable behaviors that candidates must demonstrate and assessors must observe. Scoring rubrics are the specific criteria that guide both the candidate's and the assessor's route to successful program completion. They identify the precise point on a rating scale where observed teacher behaviors can be marked. Scoring rubrics blaze the trail to reliably documented measurements that describe precisely how well each candidate performs on each established performance standard. Well-developed scoring rubrics transform an observer's subjective opinions of how well a candidate is doing or has performed into an assessor's set of objective data that document each candidate's performance outcomes.

Developing good rubrics takes practice and requires precision. To test the precision of rubrics as they are developed, it is helpful to ask, "What does that mean? What does that look like?" For example, a rubric that defines acceptable task performance as "usually demonstrates" does not tell us what "usually" means. With such ambiguously defined criteria, it is impossible to establish objectivity. Without objectivity, we cannot state with confidence that a candidate has demonstrated competent teaching skills.

Example from Florida's Assessment System

A detailed example from the standards-based assessment system used by Florida's Alternative Certification Program illustrates the specificity needed to ensure consistent objective evidence to use in making diagnostic decisions regarding the adequacy of each program candidate's performance. The example provided in Figures 5.1 and 5.2—"Task 1.5.1: Demonstrating Positive Student Outcomes"—also illustrates how the candidate's performance is directly linked to student achievement.

In Figure 5.1, both the candidate and the assessor can see the alignment of the task with specific indicators for both state and national standards. The task itself is described, along with the product that is to be submitted for scoring. Explicit instructions inform the candidate exactly what must be done to complete the task.

Figure 5.2 illustrates the scoring rubric for each aspect of the task, noting the precise criteria that the assessor will use to determine if each task element has been completed at an "acceptable," "marginal," or "unacceptable" level. Additionally, the criteria for compiling a composite rating are included

Figure 5.1   Assessment: Assessment System Product/Performance Tasks

---

Task Number: 1.5.1
Task Name: Demonstration of Positive Student Outcomes (Product)

Florida Educator   1.01, 1.04, 1.07, 1.11
Accomplished Practice Indicators:

INTASC Indicators: 8.02, 8.06, 8.09, 8.10

Task Description
The teacher demonstrates a positive impact on student learning in a major specified unit using multiple measures to determine mastery of objectives by individual students and the class as a whole.

What to Submit?
Submit a report that includes a quantitative and qualitative analysis of student learning. (End of unit/semester achievement is compared to pre-assessment results.)

Directions
To complete this task, you should do the following:
1. Choose a unit to use for this assessment task. Make sure your selection will have pre-assessment information to use in your comparison.
2. Identify the assessments (pre and post) that you will analyze, making sure that you cover all of the major outcomes you taught.
3. Create a folder that contains the unit plan (with learning outcomes) and assessments (both traditional and alternative).
4. Write an analysis of student outcomes (preferably at the goal level) for both individuals and the whole class and a summary of changes to be made as a result of the analysis. The analysis you place in your folder should include the following:
   - A summary of what students knew prior to instruction.
   - Identification of which students have mastered which learning outcomes, based on your definitions of mastery of each outcome (e.g., a test score of x% combined with an alternative assessment score of x%).
   - The number/percent of students mastering each outcome.
   - Identification of any disparities in performance for sub-groups (e.g., minorities, Limited English Proficient, Exceptional Student Education, etc.).
   - A description of strengths and weaknesses that have surfaced in student learning.
   - A description of strategies for improving instruction for next year and/or for providing any needed remediation this year for individuals and the class as a whole.
   - Identification of any changes needed in the assessments for next year.

Source: © Copyright 2002, Florida Department of Education.

to explain how the assessor will determine whether the overall task has been completed to one of three levels:

- "Demonstrated": Approximately 67% of the individual task criteria are rated as "Acceptable" with none rated as "Not Acceptable"
- "Partially Demonstrated": Less than 67% of the individual task criteria are rated as "Acceptable," but none are rated as "Unacceptable"
- "Not Demonstrated": One or more criteria are rated as "Unacceptable"

Well-developed scoring rubrics demand a logical next step. What highway markers guide the assessor to a determination of whether or not the candidate

Figure 5.2   Task 1.5.1: Demonstration of Positive Student Outcomes

Name: _____   Submission #: ____

Decision for F.E.A.P. on this Task (check one):

☐ Demonstrated: 8 or more ratings are acceptable; none are unacceptable.

☐ Partially Demonstrated: 5 to 12 ratings are marginal; none are unacceptable.

☐ Not Demonstrated: 1 or more ratings are unacceptable.

View an explanation of the rating scale.

Rating Scale Key: A = acceptable;   M = marginal;   U = unacceptable

Element	#	Criteria for "acceptable" rating	Rating
Unit plan	1	A unit plan with outcomes and the pre- and post-assessment instruments are included in the folder.	__A__M__U
Analysis of results	2	Pre-assessments are analyzed and identify what students (individuals and group) knew prior to instruction.	__A__M__U
	3	Post-assessments (including both traditional and alternative) provide valid data on progress of students toward learning the outcomes.	__A__M__U
	4	Data are presented at the student and group levels.	__A__M__U
	5	Mastery criteria are established and are reasonable.	__A__M__U
	6	Progress of individuals toward meeting the teacher's determined level of mastery is reported.	__A__M__U
	7	Progress of the group toward meeting the teacher's determined level of mastery is reported.	__A__M__U
	8	Any disparate performance of subgroups is identified.	__A__M__U
	9	Strengths and weaknesses in mastery are described appropriately.	__A__M__U
Improvement	10	Strategies for enhancing instruction next year are described and are reasonable.	__A__M__U
	11	Suggestions for enhancing the assessments next year are described and are reasonable.	__A__M__U
	12	Strategies for providing remedial instruction for individuals and the class are described and are appropriate and reasonable.	__A__M__U

Source: © Copyright 2002, Florida Department of Education.

adequately demonstrated the entire Educator Practice of Assessment? Furthermore, how does the assessor know if the candidate's overall performance throughout all 12 practices meets the requirements of competence for certification? A system of summative decision-making propels our accumulated rubric scores to the ultimate destination of a competency determination for each candidate.

Summative Decision Making

We have seen how precisely developed scoring rubrics establish the set of road markers that guide our journey with confidence and clarity down the road toward successful program completion. New questions now arise as we get closer to making a final competency determination. Can candidate assessors depend on their own expertise to conclude that a candidate will, in fact, be an effective teacher? How many of the essential teaching practices must each teacher master? To what degree of quality must each teaching practice be demonstrated? The answers to these questions are embedded in a system of summative decision making. Serving as the legend for our assessment map, the summative decision-making system defines the actual number of miles that each candidate must travel and at what rate of speed to achieve the final determination of success.

A Series of Decisions

As with each step in developing our assessment system, the standards for the common core of teacher knowledge signal the starting point in establishing the summative decision-making system. We must make a series of substrata decisions leading up to an overall decision of either successful program completion or that an individual candidate's performance is too questionable to clear the way for full certification as a professional teacher. How many skills for each competency, demonstrated to what degree of satisfactory performance, must the assessor measure to make the overall determination that a program candidate has demonstrated effectiveness in supporting successful student achievement? How do we know a candidate is competent overall to meet state certification requirements?

One thing is for certain. If we determine that all candidates perform exceptionally well, we must be living in Lake Wobegon, where, to paraphrase Garrison Keeler, "all [teachers] are above average." But, in fact, we do not live in Lake Wobegon, no matter how creative our teacher recruiters may be in attracting talented individuals to the teaching field. By establishing a system for making summative assessment decisions on the overall performance of program candidates, we can see clearly and objectively who is outstanding, who shows great promise, and who really would not be an effective teacher.

Furthermore, such a system provides program managers a quantifiable pattern of data, collected objectively and fairly by consistently applying the same criteria to all participants, to support the ultimate determination that each individual candidate either does, or does not, have what it takes to be certified as a professional teacher.

A Systematic Process

To establish a systematic method of making summative decisions regarding candidates' performance, we take the following steps:

- Start with the standards that define teacher competency, that is, the core of the program.
- Identify the set of skills and teacher behaviors you want to see for each standard of competence.
- Develop the sets of scoring rubrics for each skill and behavior that is expected as demonstration of each competency standard.
- Determine the combination of scores representing the percentage of successful performance behaviors that you absolutely must see to decide that each competency has been adequately demonstrated.
- Identify the combination of scores representing the percentage of performance behaviors that you absolutely must see to decide that the beginning level of teacher competence has been demonstrated (i.e., the level required for certification). Scoring at this level or above qualifies the candidate for certification. Scoring below this cutoff point indicates either that the candidate should not be issued a teaching certificate or that considerably more training is essential before this candidate can demonstrate overall competence as a teacher.

A Common Misconception

Here it is not only helpful but crucial to note an example of what *does not* constitute a summative decision as to whether or not a candidate has successfully completed an alternative certification program. One of the most common misconceptions of "program completion" is to assume that if a candidate has finished a series of training modules, the candidate has therefore successfully completed the alternative certification program. This would simply constitute "seat time" compliance, and in no way would it provide objective evidence of teaching competency. Likewise, seat time through completion of training modules would not demonstrate a candidate's effectiveness in producing student learning. Once again, without a systematic collection of evidence that a candidate can effectively support student achievement, we can only conclude "So what?" regarding the effectiveness of the alternative certification program.

A Four-Tiered System

In the previous section on scoring rubrics, we examined an example of one task that was selected from a total of five tasks developed to provide a representative sample of a candidate's critical skills in the Educator Accomplished Practice of Assessment. We saw how criteria were established for scoring each critical element of the sample "Task 1.5.1: Demonstration of Positive Student Outcomes," as well as the quantifiable process for producing a cumulative score to indicate how well the candidate performed on the entire task. That sample task was one of a total of five tasks, however, selected to cover the depth and breadth of the Educator Accomplished Practice of Assessment. How will the assessor determine if the candidate adequately performs the overall teaching practice of Assessment?

From here, a third level of criteria in the example from *Florida's Alternative Certification Program* leads the assessor to an objective decision of whether the candidate adequately completed the gamut of skills represented by all five of the tasks in the area of assessment. The third tier of decisions results in one comprehensive determination of "Accomplished," "Competent," or "Not Competent" on the overall practice. In the summative decision-making system, these terms are defined and calculated as follows:

- *Accomplished:* The candidate has successfully demonstrated the Educator Accomplished Practice of Assessment with repeated ratings of "Demonstrated," not more than one rating of "Partially Demonstrated," and no ratings of "Not Demonstrated" on any of the individual tasks.
- *Competent:* The candidate has adequately demonstrated the Practice, with no ratings of "Not Demonstrated." However, some performance gaps are identified by two or more ratings of "Partially Demonstrated." These gaps can be addressed through professional development plans.
- *Not Competent:* The candidate has not demonstrated minimal competence in this Practice. This has been documented by one or more ratings of "Not Demonstrated," even after additional attempts to produce the expected product correctly.

Finally, a fourth level of decision-making criteria exists in Florida's system to document and support a summative decision on whether or not the candidate has performed adequately throughout all 12 of the Educator Accomplished Practices. Quite simply, the candidate must achieve ratings of "Accomplished" or "Competent" on each of the 12 Educator Accomplished Practices for successful completion of the alternative certification program. A candidate who scores even one "Not Competent" rating on one practice has not successfully completed the program. This criterion was established from the determination that *all* of the 12 teacher practices are equally critical to effective teaching that results in successful student learning. With a similar system of explicitly defined, objective criteria that link teacher performance with student outcomes, an alternative certification program manager can clearly document an educationally meaningful response to the essential question of "So what?"

Performance-Based Assessment Instruments

Let's examine the job-related performance tasks that make up the assessment system. An essential feature of an effective assessment system is the use of multiple data sources for documenting performance. Remember that candidate assessment is not only focusing on the teacher in the classroom but the impact of the teacher's performance on student learning in the classroom. In fact, what is of primary importance in the outcomes of a standards-based assessment system is student learning and understanding, not what the teacher does or says. In addition, no matter what assessment method is used, strong consideration must always be given to the uniqueness of each classroom context in which teaching and learning occur.

Perhaps the most common method of evaluating teacher performance is based on direct observation of the teacher in the classroom using a clinical supervision model consisting of preconference, observation, and postconference. However, even though reliance on classroom observation can provide significant data about the teacher's performance and student learning, it can be too limited. Moreover, sole reliance on formal classroom observation can be problematic in that it consists of such a small sample of performance and it may have aspects of artificiality. The use of multiple data sources to measure teacher performance and its impact on student learning can result in a more comprehensive and accurate view of the quality of teaching and learning in the classroom. In addition, the integration of multiple data sources can offer a more realistic picture of actual teacher performance than would be possible if the assessment system is based solely on classroom observations.

In designing, developing, and implementing a standards-based assessment system, keep in mind the importance of multiple sources of data in designing assessment instruments for measuring teacher performance and its effect on student learning. Two data sources for teacher performance are discussed in the following section: classroom-based observations and performance-based "product" tasks and portfolios.

Classroom-Based Observations

Classroom-based observation instruments are designed to identify characteristics of effective teachers. To be a useful part of any assessment system, observations must be systematic, objective, selective, unobtrusive, and carefully recorded. Many observation instruments include checklists of specific well-defined behaviors or characteristics to be observed. Often they include rating scales to assist the observer in making judgments about a behavior or performance. Across the United States there is a proliferation of evaluation instruments designed for direct classroom observations that gather data to make judgments about effective teaching. Many localities mandate the use of a specific observation instrument for evaluating teachers. However, these instruments often have limitations in assessing both teaching and student learning performance. These include, among others: (1) the length and frequency of observations needed to make reliable judgments; (2) the role of the observer in the classroom and the intrusiveness of the observer; and (3) the number of teaching behaviors and scoring criteria necessary and sufficient to make valid judgments about competence. Many educator preparation programs use the observation instruments already in place at the institution or locality. However, it is important to review the standards that are the underpinnings of your assessment system and to identify which behaviors and skills are observable and which ones are more suited to other forms of evaluation. For instance, in the previous example of Florida's standard on Assessment, "The pre-professional teacher collects and uses data gathered from a variety of sources. . . . The teacher can identify and match the students' instructional plans with their cognitive, social, linguistic, cultural, emotional, and physical needs." An assessor, such as the school's principal, would not necessarily observe this standard in a typical classroom observation and would need to gain this information and assess the teacher's performance on this standard using other means.

Performance-Based "Product" Tasks and Portfolios

A performance-based "product" task is a job-related measure of a teacher's skills or knowledge that will ultimately impact student learning. The "product," for instance a lesson or unit plan, a resource folder, a portfolio of artifacts, or student achievement data, has tangible results. Florida's assessment system has developed 36 products, in addition to several classroom-based observation instruments, to assess all of the critical aspects of each of the 12 Educator Accomplished Practices. Each assessment task has several components:

- *Task Description:* A brief summary of what the task is about, including the product that must be submitted for evaluation
- *Standards Alignment:* The specific key indicators that each task has been correlated to for the specific Practice (both state and national)
- *Directions:* Detailed instructions that should maximize the preservice or beginning teachers' chances to produce a quality product
- *Rubric:* A scaled scoring form with descriptions of specific performance criteria on which the product will be assessed

In Figures 5.1 and 5.2, an example of a "product" task in Florida's program is depicted.

Portfolios

Portfolios are popular tools for teacher evaluation systems, and Florida's assessment system of "tasks" form the basis for a portfolio. Portfolios can be useful tools for presenting authentic views of learning and teaching over time, thus offering a complete picture of what teachers know and can do. However, if portfolios are to be used as part of an assessment system, they must be explicitly linked to the performance-based standards that form the foundation of the assessment system. In addition, consistency should be maintained in the specific requirements for the portfolio contents and how it will be evaluated (Wilkerson & Lang, 2003).

The following are suggestions when program developers are considering using a portfolio approach in a performance-based assessment system:

- Define the specific expectations for teacher performance, including student outcomes.
- Clarify the purposes for the portfolio, for example, for evaluative purposes.
- Identify the specific products with content standards that should be included in the portfolio.
- Develop guidelines for format and construction of the portfolio.
- Establish objective, consistent procedures for portfolio evaluation.

Assessor Training

How do you assure that those who are responsible for assessing candidates in alternative route programs have the skills and concepts to remain objective, fair, and free from bias? Establishing a comprehensive training program for assessors is one way to help ensure that the effective standards-based evaluative program has been appropriately implemented and will yield results that will assist in the promotion of the professional development of teachers and improved student outcomes. In Florida, a comprehensive online training tool for assessors was developed that could be utilized for any assessment system being implemented within the school districts that dealt with teacher evaluation. This training program addressed an overall understanding and purpose for assessment, including a review of the essential key concepts of a sound evaluative system: validity, reliability, and fairness. In addition, detailed instruction and practice in scoring rubrics, critical to assuring the consistency and objectivity of an assessor's formative and summative decisions regarding a teacher's performance, was developed. Multiple practice samples were included in the training to promote the interrater reliability of assessors and bias-free decisions. The training is available via the Internet so it is accessible at all times and in any location, and permits the developers easily to revise, update, and improve the training at any time, including adding more practice samples.

Data Collection for System Improvement

Any type of assessment inherently involves a cyclical process of feedback and continuous improvement. Whether the assessment is the one used by the teacher to gauge the level of student achievement or the system used to document the alternative certification candidate's acquisition of essential teaching competencies, the assessment system itself must be routinely evaluated. Regular and systematic data collection and analysis are basic to the process of continuous improvement.

The infrastructure map for evaluation of an alternative certification program's candidate assessment system has already been laid. From an accepted core of teacher knowledge, standards for essential teaching competencies have been developed. The essential teaching competencies have been aligned with standards for student achievement. The essential teaching competencies have been broken down into discrete skills that can be observed throughout the student learning process. A system of scoring rubrics has been developed to establish the level of achievement expected and an objective scale for documenting each candidate's skill demonstration. A corollary system of decision making has also been developed to incorporate all of the results from the scoring rubrics into a series of summative decisions that determine whether the candidate's overall performance meets acceptable, exceptional, or unacceptable standards for certification. Finally, a system of collecting and analyzing the summative data from each group of program candidates produces feedback on the effectiveness of the candidate assessment system itself. Such a system can also provide one source of feedback for use in evaluating the overall effectiveness of the alternative certification program.

A Database of Assessment Decisions

One familiar model—the bell curve—is useful in understanding the importance of assessing the alternative certification program's candidate assessment system. Just as the bell curve is useful to a teacher in determining whether or not a test has been an effective tool in the learning process, so too can it be useful in gaining an overview of the effectiveness of the candidate assessment system. A database into which all of the candidate assessment data can be readily and routinely entered is invaluable.

By clustering the skills that comprise each essential teaching competency within the group of competencies that comprise each major topic of core teaching knowledge, alternative certification program managers can see at a glance how well the system of scoring rubrics is working to identify (1) the majority of candidates who should perform at the designated "acceptable" level, compared with (2) the smaller number of candidates who perform at the "exceptional" level, as well as (3) the very few candidates whose overall performance fell too short of the mark to meet the minimum level of achievement required for certification.

If *all* candidates' performances are rated as "exceptional," one or more elements of the candidate assessment system need fine tuning. Remember, despite the success and creativity of our program recruiters to bring in the very best candidates, we do not live in Lake Wobegon. If everyone is rated as "exceptional," then "exceptional" has lost its meaning. Consequently, our candidate assessment system is not effectively serving its most basic purpose to protect the public by ensuring that all who successfully complete the program do so by demonstrating at least the entry level of competence required for state certification. Program managers must take note and make systemic program adjustments.

On the flip side, if an inordinate number of candidates scored as "unacceptable," then something is amiss in the program. Although this could indicate that our recruiters have tapped into a population that simply is not suited to the teaching profession, the more likely implications are either that our candidate assessment system is not resulting in a valid picture of each individual's skills and competencies or our program curriculum is not appropriately aligned with the standards for teaching competencies. Other perspectives for data analysis can reveal whether or not individual assessment tasks may unintentionally discriminate against protected populations of candidates. Regardless, any such data would clearly tell us that we need to examine our assessment system at a ground level for starters. Possibly other elements of our alternative certification program should be scrutinized to ensure that the system is founded on essential ingredients of a sound assessment system, as well as alignment throughout the assessment system and the program curriculum with standards for both teaching competencies and student learning.

Indicators of Individual Task Difficulty

Another facet of a systematic means of assessing our program's candidate assessment system provides us with a microscopic view of the difficulty level of each assessment task. We can view our database of assessment ratings from the perspective of how our candidates perform overall on each skill in the clusters of skills that we have identified as a valid demonstration of each essential teaching competency. Are some assessment tasks too difficult? Are there some tasks that incorporate other tasks, such that successful completion of one comprehensive task could take the place of other less difficult ones? This level of data analysis can be especially useful in an alternative certification program by pinpointing possible paths of competency demonstration that can be streamlined for individuals who come to the program with previous experience that translates to a shorter learning curve. As a result, this specific type of summative assessment data analysis can help managers streamline or customize their alternative certification programs for maximum efficiency and effectiveness.

Feedback on a Variety of Program Variables

Our assessment database can yield other useful feedback for program managers. By viewing assessment results from the perspective of individual candidates or from the overall results of candidates grouped by any number of variables—mentors or curriculum delivery sites are two possible examples—a program manager can see if any unusual differences stand out. If one group of candidates appears to be performing significantly better or achieving successful results more quickly than other candidate groups, perhaps the peer who is mentoring or the person who is delivering training to that group is using more effective mentoring or training techniques. If so, then let's see what is happening with that group so we can transfer the more productive strategies to other areas of our program.

By all means, we want to discover whatever can positively impact our ultimate goal of certifying teachers who have successfully demonstrated the competencies necessary for highest student achievement. Including a database of task, practice, and summative data decisions that can be cross-referenced with a variety of candidate information can be invaluable in a process of continuous improvement.

Systematic collection and analysis of all assessment data can ensure one final layer of professionalism to support a solid response, based on objective, quantifiable evidence, to the ultimate question of "So what? Is our alternative certification program simply a smorgasbord of delivery options for teacher training curriculum through nontraditional paths? Or does our program epitomize a truly successful strategy for producing highly competent teachers who are effective in ensuring highest student learning?" A standards-based response, bolstered with a well-defined system of evidence, passes the litmus test of "So what?" and lands your alternative certification program squarely on the bull's-eye of success.

Conclusion

Florida, like many other states, is struggling to meet the ever-growing demand for highly qualified teachers for its classrooms. As a result, Florida responded to the high demand for teachers by mandating that all school districts offer an alternative route to teacher certification for qualified individuals. As a part of this alternative route, Florida created and implemented a standards-based assessment system for its district alternative certification programs on July 1, 2002. Since that time, the Florida Department of Education has been committed to continual improvement of its programs, overall, and its ability to support district-developed programs, including its assessment systems. As a result, Florida has learned many lessons that may be helpful to other alternate route providers who are just beginning or seeking ways to improve their systems. The following is a sample of what Florida has learned from its experiences.

Legally Defensible Assessment System

A legally defensible assessment system must stand on three pillars: validity, reliability, and fairness. Because of the complexity of assessment issues that arise when developing an evaluative system, we strongly recommend that experts in the field of assessment or psychometrics be procured to assist. In Florida, the state department of education, in collaboration with researchers at the University of South Florida (USF) St. Petersburg, generated assessment criteria for districts to use when designing legally defensible assessment systems. With guidance from the measurement experts, a standards-based assessment system was developed that would require new teachers to demonstrate the knowledge and skills associated with each of Florida's Educator Accomplished Practices. In addition, the measurement experts assisted Florida in a series of studies to support the validity of teacher certification decisions that were integral to the assessment system. The results of these studies provided solid support for the assessment tasks that are part of *Florida's Alternative Certification Program* as a collection of evidence useful for determining the competency of teacher candidates seeking a professional teaching certificate in Florida.

Resistance to Change

Many people who begin to design an assessment system rely on measures that are already in place, whether it is in a teacher preparation program within an institution or within a school district. That has been true in Florida as well. Although Florida mandated that school districts must offer an alternative certification route that is standards based, it was difficult for many districts to comprehend fully the importance of aligning the state's standards (Educator Accomplished Practices) to the assessment instrument(s). For years school districts had been relying solely on performance measurement systems that exclusively used an evaluative instrument(s) that depended heavily on observation in the classroom. Because many of the educator standards are unobservable behaviors or skills, teacher performance was being inadequately evaluated and measured.

In working with school districts, the Florida Department of Education required school districts who were not using the state-developed assessment system to submit documentation of each component of their assessment system and to demonstrate its alignment to Florida's 12 standards, down to the level of key specific indicators. To meet specifications for an approved program, the district had to demonstrate that its assessment system addressed all 12 Educator Accomplished Practices—not just one time, but more than once—and that multiple specific key indicators were addressed for each standard.

This was a time-consuming task for some of the school districts but well worth the time in verifying the alignment of their assessment system to the standards. If gaps were identified in the assessment system, the school district was required to create, adapt, or adopt other measures that would fill in the holes.

Strategies for Improvement

In developing a legally defensible assessment system, great emphasis must be placed on the development (or insurance) of an integrated system that contains multiple data sources that can offer a more realistic picture of actual teacher performance. It has been a challenging experience to convince school district officials that a new system needed to be developed that would more accurately measure teacher performance, particularly as it pertained to student performance outcomes. Florida required each school district to ensure the alignment of its assessment system with the standards. Moreover, school districts had to demonstrate that each standard was being measured in multiple ways, with a variety of sources, and over a period of time to demonstrate the depth and breadth of their system. In addition, the development of scoring rubrics for each measure was strongly encouraged and supported. As a result, district assessment systems for alternatively prepared teachers have dramatically improved, moving them ever closer to a sound and legally defensible system of evaluation.

Emphasis on Training

Assessment systems are the key to successful alternate educator preparation programs. Even though local systems have implemented extensive training of those who will ultimately decide whether a teacher is competent or not, other personnel, including peer mentors, are also an integral part of understanding and implementing the assessment system. Florida has learned that critical and key concepts of a standards-based assessment system must be repeatedly emphasized and that assessors need multiple opportunities to practice their skills in objective decision making. In fact, there never can be too much training when it comes to preparing an effective assessor. As a result, Florida's development of a dynamic online training program to assist its assessors in fine-tuning their skills has been a critical piece in assuring a legitimate system of assessment is in place.

References

Florida Department of Education. (2004, February). *Analysis of district coordinators' validity questionnaire of assessment tasks.* Tallahassee: Author.

Florida Department of Education. *Competencies for teachers of the 21st century* [Brochure]. Tallahassee: Author.

Florida Department of Education. (2002). *Florida's alternative certification program.* Retrieved May 1, 2006, from http://www.altcertflorida.org

Gronlund, N.E. (1993). *How to make achievement tests and assessments* (5th ed.). Needham Heights, MA: Allyn & Bacon.

Slatterly, W. (2006). *Assessment.* Retrieved April 26, 2006, from The National Science Digital Library, Science Education Resource Center at Carlton College Website, http://serc.carleton.edu/introgeo/assessment/scorerubrics.html

Wilkerson, J.R., & Lang, W.S. (2003, December 3). Portfolios, the Pied Piper of teacher certification assessments: Legal and psychometric issues. *Education Policy Analysis Archives, 11*(45). Retrieved June 7, 2006, from http://epaa.asu.edu/epaa/v11n45/

6

❧

Management of Alternate Route Teacher Certification Programs

Michael McKibbin
California Commission on Teacher Credentialing

*F*or more than 20 years, California has encouraged the development of alternative routes to certification (ARC). For the past 13 years the state has invested in this type of teacher preparation and certification by providing grants to school districts, county offices of education, and colleges and universities to provide ARC services. In that period of time, nearly 100 programs have operated. I have had the opportunity to interact with each of these programs over that period. Each year the programs have provided reports on their successes, challenges, and lessons learned. Annual meetings, interviews, and site visits have provided opportunities to reflect on these lessons from the field.

In this chapter I summarize what those program directors have taught me about ARC. I summarize those areas that seem to have made the greatest differences as we have prepared nearly 40,000 teachers in the past 13 years to work in California's most challenging schools. The chapter focuses on the lessons that have been learned about ARC program management and offers tips and techniques about ARC program start-up and implementation.

Managing Alternative Route Certification Programs

Managing an ARC program is like managing any other system, company, school, or group of people. Listening is more important than talking. Asking questions is more important than giving answers. Managing an alternative route may be a bit more like managing a business than a school or other teacher preparation program because most ARC programs are market sensitive. The programs are usually driven by principles of supply and demand. On the supply side, the clients are the teachers who will be prepared. The supply advantage of programs is that they can target persons who might not otherwise enter teaching, such as second-career professionals. On the demand side, school districts need the candidates that ARC programs provide to fill teaching vacancies and to bring to their classrooms the unique talents of those who have been recruited. It is the task of the program director and the management team to develop a teacher transition program that builds a bridge between the supply side and the demand side.

A manager of an ARC program must first determine how much or, in most cases, how little he or she has control over. The best strategy is to ask a series of questions. Some of these questions the manager will ask of himself or herself. Some questions will be asked of those to whom the manager is responsible, some of the work team, and the remainder of the clients: the district employers and the potential teachers. Among the questions that should be asked are the following:

> What are we (the program partners) trying to accomplish? What are our goals?
> How do we make this program effective?
> How do we best communicate what we do to others?
> How do we reach our goals?
> What skills and experiences do you (as director, teacher, support provider) bring with you to teaching and this alternative route program?

These questions are not complicated, but they need to be asked to lay the foundation for an ARC program.

Determining the Goals of the ARC Program

Across the country, alternative routes to certification are usually implemented to reach one or more of four goals. These goals form the foundation for the strategies used to recruit and select participants, implement the instructional program, employ a support system, and develop partnerships. The primary goals of the ARC programs should drive all other decisions.

Goal 1: Assist Districts in Meeting Their Need for Teachers

Across the country the most frequent reason that alternative routes are implemented is to help school districts meet their needs for teachers. Two recent studies in California have shown that 80% of ARC teachers are employed in the hardest-to-staff schools. These are the schools located in regions that have the highest rates of poverty, show the lowest student achievement scores, and are located in the most geographically isolated districts. In many cases if fully certificated teachers were available to teach in these high-need districts, ARC programs would not be necessary.

ARC programs tend to organize themselves to meet teaching market demand. For example, in 1997 in California, the legislature and governor passed the California Class Size Initiative. This program created an instant shortage of 18,000 elementary teachers because class size was reduced in the lowest four grades from an average ratio of 32:1 to 20:1. For the next 7 years, ARC programs were the primary method used to close the supply gap for elementary teachers. Nine years later the demand has been met. As of this writing (2006–2007), programs to prepare elementary teachers are now the smallest proportion of ARC programs. For the past 3 years, ARC programs for special education teachers have become the largest group. Seventy percent of the secondary ARC teachers teach the three subjects with the greatest need: English, mathematics, and science. In 2005, more than half of California's math teachers were prepared through ARC programs.

Although the other goals listed later may be featured in an ARC program, the demand for teachers by the districts in the program's service area likely will drive the program. This goal cannot be met with any precision without accurate data. A system to collect accurate data from every partnering district about teacher demand is critical. Program managers will find that their ability to adjust to the needs of partnering districts will be among the assets that will help the program thrive and be a primary reason why the candidates of the program will be requested by the partnering districts.

ARC programs in California serve an incredible range of more than 800 school districts. The programs serve some of the largest districts in the country. For example, 29 of the ARC programs in the state have candidates teaching in the Los Angeles Unified School District, one of the largest school districts in the country. But ARC programs also serve some of the most rural and isolated districts in the state. There are ARC teachers in districts along the desert regions of Southern California and in the alpine regions of the northeast where there are hundreds of rural isolated districts. When a school has lost its mathematics or special education teacher in a district that has 100 or fewer students in the rural regions of California, it is likely that without an ARC teacher, there will be no other qualified choice. Issues of demand may be quite different in these geographic locations, but the need is no less crucial. ARC programs need to be customized and configured to meet whatever demands their service area requires.

Goal 2: Expand the Pool of Qualified Teachers

The second most frequent goal across the country is to expand the pool of qualified teachers by attracting into teaching those people who might not otherwise enter the classroom. Traditional teacher preparation programs are usually designed for college undergraduates or recent graduates. These programs are characterized by subject matter and pedagogical studies followed by a student teaching experience in which the novice teacher is apprenticed to an experienced teacher in a school near the college or university offering the program. The programs provide a graduated set of instructional and field experiences to assist the potential teacher learn the craft and professional aspects of teaching. The student teacher is assigned to a veteran teacher who guides the novice through a graduated set of increasingly complex teaching experiences, leading eventually to whole-class solo experiences in the veteran teacher's classroom. In most circumstances this model has been a successful method to bring young adults into teaching. The student teaching–based route has historically produced the majority of our nation's teachers. It is a route particularly well suited for young adults who will benefit from a graduated series of experiences and serve in an apprentice mode under a master teacher.

The term *traditional teacher preparation program* is not meant to be at all negative, but it is the term used as a contrast to ARC programs. When I use the term *traditional teacher preparation,* I am referring to any model that includes, as its primary field experience, a student teacher/master teacher situation. Both traditional and ARC programs have an important role in providing high-quality teachers. There are many variations among traditional routes. In the 40-plus states that offer undergraduate education majors, it has been the primary route into teaching. Yet many of these states have added the option of a postbaccalaureate education major route to accommodate those who decide they want to be teachers later in their lives.

Alternative routes to teacher certification have a unique opportunity in teacher recruitment and preparation. Because of the way programs are configured, ARC can bring persons into teaching who probably would not enter teaching. Managers of an ARC program should capitalize on this program feature. The critics of ARC programs frequently or conveniently ignore the possibility that there is a unique market supply niche for ARC programs. Among those potential teachers that ARC programs have been able to serve across the country are the following groups that seem particularly well suited for the ARC preparation and support model.

Second-Career Professionals   Over the years I have talked to dozens, maybe even hundreds, of persons who said, "I always wanted to be a teacher, but . . ." Sometimes the words that followed the "but" were that a university adviser, often in their content area, said something like, "You are too smart to be a teacher." Other times a family member would say, "Why do you want to be a teacher? You can't make any money doing that." But after some time working in another profession, that calling was still there. However, economic forces, such as family obligations, would preclude them from taking a year or so off to enter a traditional student teaching–based program.

Because an ARC program allows people to enter teaching without forgoing earnings for that year, they have a chance to achieve this life goal. For others, teaching provides an opportunity to give back to the community. These individuals are at a place in their lives when they want to apply the lessons they have learned from their life experiences and make them available to children or youth. This does not mean these life experiences are all that are necessary to teach, but rather that these second-career professionals are well positioned to enter a teacher preparation program that takes full advantage of prior experiences and fills in the learning gaps through an alternative teacher preparation program.

Special Population Recruitment Another feature of ARC programs is targeted recruitment. Across the country, ARC programs report that they have been able to focus their recruitment efforts on segments of the population underrepresented in the teaching workforce. For the last 10 years in California, those from ethnic and racial groups underrepresented in the teaching workforce have constituted half of the ARC candidates, which is twice the rate of representation of underrepresented ethnic and racial groups in the current teaching workforce. Fourteen percent of the special education teachers nationwide are men, whereas in California in the past 3 years, 32% of the ARC special education students have been male. ARC programs have recognized this inequity and have consciously focused their efforts on bringing men into special education classrooms. A similar story could be told about elementary classrooms. Particularly interesting is the number of former military personnel (most of whom are men) who are choosing to serve in elementary classrooms.

Program directors point out several reasons why they have been successful in recruiting those underrepresented in the teaching workforce. One reason is changing attitudes. The directors found ways to make it acceptable for a man to teach in a profession traditionally held by women. They did this by citing the importance of male role models in educating the whole child. If diversifying the teaching workforce is important to the partners being served by the ARC program, targeted recruitment may in the long run become the most important goal with the most lasting effect for ARC programs.

Many of the program directors have branched out into other areas of recruitment. Special education ARC programs have found a recruitment audience in parents of students with disabilities and students with disabilities themselves as excellent candidates for ARC programs. Their life experiences have brought them a vast amount of knowledge that will help them move expeditiously through a teacher preparation program. Similarly, paraprofessionals bring years of experience with children. As one person I talked to said, "There is very little about classrooms and students that will surprise a teacher's aide." More and more schools are requesting that parents spend time in classrooms. Many ARC program directors now actively recruit these parents, particularly as their children get older and feelings about their empty nests may motivate these parents to seek another kind of fulfillment that teaching can bring.

As noted earlier, in the last 2 years nearly half of the math teachers who have become teachers in California have been prepared through ARC programs. There is still a great shortage, but ARC has made a dent. One reason for the shortage is that not enough undergraduates are majoring in math for the vacancies available in all areas of employment. ARC programs have come to realize that the type of program they offer is quite attractive to many of those who have taken their mathematics expertise and used it in corporate America. Second-career mathematics teachers tell us that after a few years, their jobs had changed from using their knowledge of mathematics to becoming more managerial. For those with a deep affinity for their subject, many are turning to another career—teaching—so they can use their skills and knowledge of mathematics in a meaningful way.

A Note of Caution   For those who come into teaching from second careers or later in life, demonstrating subject-matter knowledge is more difficult than they expected. For example, there was an economic slump for the high-technology industries of California, a large number of engineers sought employment as teachers, particularly as mathematics teachers. Many failed the state's mathematics exam. Upon further review, it was discovered that for many of the engineers, their collegiate preparation in mathematics quickly became specific and focused on those areas germane to their engineering discipline rather than more broadly focused as would be needed by a high school mathematics teacher.

In other cases, such as in areas of science, the prospective teachers' knowledge was showing some age because so much had changed since their collegiate days. Managers of ARC programs who seek to include second-career professionals in programs need to be aware of the possibility that not all who come to teaching will qualify. Strategies such as test preparation assistance should be built into the recruitment and hiring process of subject-matter experts to make it completely successful. Providing exploratory experiences for second-career professionals are also wise. Some candidates do not realize how much the schools of today differ from the schools of their childhood.

Client-Customized Teacher Preparation   Another reason that ARC programs are seen as attractive to many teachers is because traditional teacher preparation may have a negative reputation. Many, like myself, who have spent many years around classrooms and teacher preparation programs believe that a good deal of the criticisms that describe teacher preparation as "Mickey Mouse," "unscientific," or worse, think that these criticisms are at best undeserved or offered by those who fail to understand the complexities of teaching. As one who believes it is more difficult to teach a child to read than to build a bridge, becoming a teacher is not for the meek or the uncommitted.

Based on my research I have observed that only one profession, air traffic controller, has to respond to more stimuli in any given hour than an elementary teacher. I know there is much to know and be able to do to be a teacher. Teacher preparation program delivery systems must be examined and customized to account for the prior experiences of the teachers who choose a particular route.

For those who have decided they want to become teachers after their initial collegiate experience and after they have entered other occupations, the student teaching–based teacher preparation model may not be well suited for them. Economic reasons may preclude those who have a family, mortgage and other financial obligations from becoming a teacher, even if they wish to move to teaching because it will provide them more personal satisfaction. For some who have spent their employed lives in jobs where learning by doing is the standard operating procedure, a traditional preparation model may not be the suitable or most effective mode of learning. ARC programs take into account the needs of their clients and provide a mode of preparation that accommodates this new category of potential teachers.

ARC programs have great potential to expand the talent pool of teachers. At the same time, we should not assume that ARC is suitable for all who desire to become a teacher. As mentioned earlier, student teaching–based teacher preparation provides graduated sets of instructional and field experiences that are developmentally well suited for undergraduate collegians. They provide exploratory experiences so these students can decide whether teaching is the right career. Teacher candidates move through a set of experiences where the student takes on more responsibility with the careful support of an experienced teacher. When executed properly, such as preparation through the professional development school model, novice teachers should emerge with the necessary solid preparation and foundation for their beginning years of teaching.

Role of Emergency Permits in California   Our experiences in California have shown that in certain circumstances ARC is problematic as a teacher preparation model. In the 1990s, hiring persons on emergency permits (EPs) who had not completed teacher preparation programs became quite normal. This was caused by a number of forces. Some districts resorted to hiring the least expensive teachers they could find when their budgets were limited by less than full funding.

Later in the 1990s, the California Class Size Initiative was passed, reducing class size virtually overnight in the lowest four grades. Districts were left with little choice but to hire less than fully prepared teachers if they were going to have teachers in every classroom. College graduates looking for employment and for ways to pay off their student loans sought teaching positions without benefit of teacher preparation and were eager to apply for positions advertised by districts. For those who were experienced products of schooling and now had a college degree with the need for a job, this opportunity seemed like a good match, at least until something better came along.

Many of these EP holders had yet to demonstrate that they knew the subjects they were teaching. Largely left to their own devices, with little support and less pedagogical preparation, these novices struggled. In the 1990s, more than two thirds of these EP holders left teaching before they achieved initial certification.

Later in the decade, California state legislation (and the federal legislation No Child Left Behind were passed to make hiring emergency teachers as the norm unacceptable. Internships, California's primary version of ARC, became the default model for districts and emergency teachers.

Lessons Learned from Emergency Certification   The negative experience that ARC programs had with EP holders led to other important lessons. ARC programs wanted to figure out what about the EP experience made these teacher candidates so problematic as interns. ARC program directors have come to realize that successfully moving EP holders to certification was a much more complicated issue than originally imagined. Through a series of interviews with EP holders, it was determined that they fell into many categories in terms of their career goals.

Category 1 Emergency Permit Holders   As many as a third of EP holders had no desire to achieve full teacher certification. For them, substitute teaching was a job that was readily available to college graduates who could pass a $40 basic skills test of reading, writing, and mathematics. Substitute teachers could make approximately $100 a day, which was significantly higher than what many alternative jobs paid. Substitute teachers could work when they wanted to. They could continue working by completing two education-related courses a year and keeping their employers happy, which usually meant showing up on time and having relatively few complaints. For persons waiting to go to graduate school or waiting for the right job to come along, it was just what they needed. For some, the experience was rewarding, and they pursued the appropriate courses and exams to enter postbaccalaureate teacher preparation. For many, particularly those thrust into very challenging situations, other career possibilities could not come soon enough.

Category 2 EP Holders　A second category of EP teachers was those that wanted to teach but could not meet a particular requirement. In most cases in California and many other states, this requirement was the demonstration of subject-matter competence at the required level. In areas like mathematics, fewer than 1 in 4 of the EP holders had sufficient subject-matter background to pass a test that tried to determine if the candidate had the equivalent of a collegiate major. Programs such as the California Pre-intern Program were developed for those who struggled with subject matter. This program was able to double the number of teachers who achieved subject-matter competence. For 6 years this program served as a main feeder for intern programs. When NCLB became the law of the land, this program was terminated because persons who were in this program did not meet the subject-matter requirements of federal law, and districts could not qualify for federal funds for those classrooms.

Local school districts continue to struggle to find potential teachers who possess subject-matter competence. Many have continued to use the strategies developed in the Pre-Intern Program. Among the strategies that were helpful for those who had been out of college for many years were refresher courses. Workshops were designed for persons who had taken appropriate coursework years before. For them, updating and upgrading that knowledge was sufficient to allow them to demonstrate the appropriate subject-matter knowledge.

In some cases, program directors found that a different kind of skill development was necessary for prospective teachers. For some prospective teachers who were unfamiliar with current testing practices, passing required tests became an insurmountable barrier. Individuals may possess the necessary knowledge but may have difficulty demonstrating that knowledge on required tests. Some even developed phobias toward testing. For these potential teachers, test-taking strategies were very valuable. Tips as simple as don't change answers unless you are sure you are changing to a correct answer, erase wrong answers completely, read the directions carefully, or make a key word outline before you start an essay proved very valuable.

A group that particularly benefited from those types of tips was persons whose first language was not English. For them the missing ingredient was often lack of confidence. For programs whose goal was to assure that all who could qualify for teaching were given every chance, this type of assistance was both consistent with their goals and beneficial to those served.

Category 3 EP Holders　The third group of EP holders that emerged was those who were interested in becoming teachers but for some reason chose not to enter a teacher preparation program. In some cases they had undergraduate preparation in a high-need content field, and school districts, desperate to fill their vacancies, hired them knowing they had gaps in their preparation. Our interviews showed that the districts that engaged in this practice were seldom fully participating in intern programs, and they often had a rather low opinion of teacher preparation programs. When these districts were offered data that showed how many EP holders did not achieve full certification, and when they were informed that there were routes, such as internships, that could help support and prepare those hired, most were quick to become ARC partners. Subsequently when the school districts found that these teachers stayed in teaching longer and were generally more skilled and happier, many districts stopped hiring EP teachers.

In some cases the EP holders would seek admission into an intern program after years of teaching on an emergency permit. This was usually the result of the EP holder being in one of these situations:

- Not being able to find the courses they needed
- Needing to be supervised to complete certification
- Finding they needed to be in a more organized, supported preparation program

Because there was a push to move persons off EP, most were able to find intern slots. However, interviews with teacher preparation program personnel provided interesting anecdotal information. Teacher preparation program directors frequently reported the difficulties they were having with former EP holders. Some teacher preparation program directors reported that remedial pedagogy was necessary. The EP holders who were left largely to their own devices and with little district or preparation program support had developed habits that were not pedagogically sound. Their management practices were sometimes based on punitive measures. Their instruction focused on those who could readily answer the questions. Their management of classroom traffic was haphazard. The preparation programs found that the time and effort to break bad habits might take two or three times the effort and time normally expected. Often these same students resented the pedagogical offerings because they saw themselves as veteran teachers without need of formal management and instructional strategies. Fortunately these cases were usually exceptions, and most of the EP holders thrived within their new support system and embraced the strategies that made them more effective.

ACPs Reduce Emergency Permits   With the assistance of federal Transition to Teaching funds, two California school districts (Oakland and San Diego) took on a project to attack the issue of EPs as a systemic problem in their districts. Each asked the question, "What would it take to reduce the use of EPs to zero?" Alternative routes to certification were integral to the success of this project. In the 3 years of the project, EP use was reduced from 560 to 12 in the two districts (a 95% reduction). The model developed is outlined here:

1. *Identify those on EPs and collect data on their circumstances.* In both districts there was no central database on who was teaching on an EP. Although the districts knew the names of the EP holders, they did not know if they were advancing toward full certification. In some cases they did not know what university they were attending. In most cases no person had ever talked to the candidates about their certification.

2. *Advise each candidate of the options available and develop a plan to achieve certification.* A credential analyst interviewed each participant. In some cases participants resisted these interventions; others were pleased that they were being assisted. Those who chose not to move toward certification were not rehired.

3. *Develop a support system for each candidate and track progress as part of the data collection system.* Each participant was assigned a mentor. Each candidate's partnering teacher preparation program was contacted and a plan was mutually developed by the participant, teacher preparation program, and the district.

4. *Develop partnerships with teacher preparation agencies to facilitate the candidate's pursuit of full certification.* In some cases no programs were available. This was the case in some low-incidence special education areas. The participants helped facilitate alternate delivery modes such as distance learning.

5. *Provide smooth transitions through each phase of the learning to teach continuum.* The goal was to move the candidates through teacher preparation, usually through internships and into an induction program. Of those that chose to proceed to become certified, 95% achieved this goal.

In this example, ARC was part of a much larger reform. The directors of the ARC programs in each district were central to the process. They provided the strategies and the positive attitudes that made it difficult for the others involved not to put in the effort to reduce EP use. Among the most satisfying aspects of this project were the changes that occurred in the ways the districts approached certification and staffing issues. The staffs of the two districts stated that they had succeeded in changing the culture around hiring in the districts. No longer was serving on an EP acceptable practice. Moving toward full certification became the norm.

As a result, an insidious pattern that allowed some of our most challenging classrooms to be taught with uncredentialed teachers was halted. This was one part in the process of supporting new teachers and investing in their success. The districts involved in this project were engaging in capacity building and building partnerships with local teacher preparation programs. An infrastructure had to be built within the district and with their preparation partners. The model that was developed was portable and was adopted by other districts.

Goal 3: Provide Experience-Based Teacher Preparation

The third most common goal for ARC programs across the country is the desire to provide a different kind of preparation program for those who want to become teachers. These preparation programs frequently capitalize on the two goals described previously. ARC preparation programs are designed to enable K–12 schools to respond immediately to pressing district needs while providing professional preparation that links education theory with classroom practice throughout each intern's preparation. The programs also have the opportunity to take advantage of the experiences and strengths that interns bring with them.

The goal of each program is to provide effective instruction, supervision, and intensive support so each alternative route candidate's learning can be targeted to individual needs. Allowing ARC teachers opportunities to extend, apply, and refine what they learn in the course of their initial preparation while serving as teacher of record adds a factor of relevance less present in most teacher preparation. Because of what ARC programs know about learning theory, particularly as it pertains to adult learners, programs develop teacher preparation programs that focus on application of teaching skills. ARC programs are asking novice teachers to learn on the job, so we must make the preparation program nimble and flexible enough to adjust to the changes and corrections that novice practitioners must make when a particular technique or strategy is not working in their classroom. In a later section on delivering instruction, more detail is provided on how to reach this goal.

One of the most positive outcomes of experience-based teacher preparation has been its ability to link instruction, support, and performance assessment. As noted before, because the ARC candidates are teachers of record, there is a sense of urgency for the instructional aspects of the program. When a teacher has to use the instructional strategies being taught almost immediately, it is truly a teachable moment. It is when instruction makes the most sense and has the greatest power.

Sequencing instruction to match the needs of the ARC candidates is very important. All those who facilitate learning must know the sequence of instruction. This includes the course instructors, the support providers, and those who are conducting performance assessment. Making sure that support providers know what segments of coursework are being taught is critical to reinforce the learning and contributes to the ability to transfer that knowledge into their own teaching.

The current set of California teacher certification structures and standards require that all candidates complete a performance assessment based on an established set of Teaching Performance Expectations (TPE). The TPE provides the layout of the knowledge, skills, and abilities that California educators determined appropriate for each beginning teacher to know and be able to do. For the past 5 years, California educators have been engaged in implementing the performance assessment system. ARC programs have led the way in implementing this reform. They report that the performance assessment is used to tie all of the pieces of the program together. It provided a way for both the program and the candidate to be measured against standards and benchmarks.

Goal 4: Develop Expedited Forms of Teacher Preparation

This fourth goal of ARC is the most controversial and problematic. It is the goal most touted by those who criticize the way that teachers are prepared in traditional teacher preparation. It is the goal most frequently mentioned by those who want to find the quickest possible route into teaching. This type of ARC is characterized by allowing individuals to test out of portions of a program or permitting certain experiences to substitute for requirements. In some states the expedited routes do not meet the same standards as either traditional or other ARC routes.

Most examples of these expedited alternative routes involve testing out or equivalence granting procedures. In California the Early Completion Intern Option allows pedagogically experienced persons to test out of nearly all of the courses that relate to how to teach. The candidates must still demonstrate subject-matter competence and competence in the teaching of reading. If they are able to meet these prerequisites, pass the Teaching Foundations Exam, which is a pedagogical skills test in their content area, and complete the state's performance assessment with the students in their classroom, they are certified to teach. This process can be completed in as little as 6 months.

There is an audience for expedited routes. These quicker routes that draw on tests and assessments have been available for nearly 4 years in California. Relatively few persons have shown an interest in this route. In discussions with potential participants, most want the support and experienced-based instruction that ARC programs offer. However, certain people can offer a solid background in working with students. For these candidates, the opportunity to test out of coursework is appropriate.

For as long as there have been teacher preparation programs, universities and other teacher preparers have the option of granting equivalence for prior experiences and courses taken in another venue. Granting equivalence has generally been underutilized by teacher preparation programs. However, ARC programs should have no interest in duplicative coursework or experience. Program directors report that more and more they are open to finding ways to allow candidates to display what they already know, and offer options to demonstrate the skills and abilities called for in our program standards. If ARC programs are standards and performance based, then ways should be found to provide expedited routes for those that desire these options. It is equally certain that expedited routes should meet the same standards of quality as both traditional and other alternative routes. If teacher preparation programs would consider using the tools that are available, such as standards-based ways of granting equivalence, many of the criticisms of these programs would be greatly reduced.

Developing Partnerships in Successful ARC Programs

ARC programs across the country have learned that the best programs are those that involve the school districts who hire the candidates in all phases of the program. The best programs operate from a philosophy that "shared power increases the power" of all participants. There are opportunities to involve district partners at every level. If a district, consortium of districts, or a university is establishing a new program, involving as many as possible potential district partners in the initial planning and goal setting will contribute to the credibility of the program. If program sponsors are adapting an existing program, those adaptations should reflect the needs of the partnering districts. For example, as a California state university and a local metropolitan district set up their ARC program, the local school district wanted to have a greater emphasis on a particular reading system. They were able to negotiate that reading program into the preservice program and into the ongoing instruction.

Selection and Hiring

In many ARC programs, both the teacher preparation program and the school districts participate in the selection and hiring processes. For example, in some programs the districts and university use the Haberman Urban Teacher Selection Interview. They have found the midrange functions of this interview have been highly predictive in which teachers will stay and succeed as teachers in very challenging environments. In other programs a locally developed instrument is used that assesses background, academic potential, and attitudes toward children, parents, and schooling. Partnering school districts appreciate highly predictive selection strategies for a number of reasons. One is that many of the selection instruments stress personal teacher responsibility for the learning of each child and other attitudes based on mutual respect sought by nearly all quality schools. Other reasons include that those who pass selection tools have a history of staying in their classrooms significantly longer than those who are selected for other reasons. Human resources departments can quantify the savings for every teacher that they do not have to replace.

Partnerships in recruitment and hiring have also had very positive results in those programs that perceive these initial phases as part of a larger process of learning to teach. For example, one of the most problematic issues is late hiring. The probability of an ARC candidate's success increases significantly if the person participates in a preservice program before becoming a teacher of record. Even urban districts with high rates of teacher fluidity can and have developed teacher demand models that can predict the teachers they need within 10%. After some years of practice, many have increased their ability to predict to even higher percentages.

Programs that use models that have high predictive validity in selection and employ these systems to gauge the demand for teachers benefit in many ways. For example, if they are able to offer contracts early, they do not have to rely on a talent pool that has been picked over. If they select teachers who come with favorable predispositions toward children and schooling, the probability of success and retention increases considerably. For those who are hired late, it is hard to avoid the feeling that the ARC candidate and those who are trying to help the candidate succeed are trying to catch up. Partnerships and joint planning for selection and hiring can make a difference in the early stages of teacher development, in the economic bottom line for the district, and in the quality of teachers who serve children.

Support and Instruction

The next phase of ARC partnerships is the support and instruction phase of teacher development. The best ARC programs view these aspects collectively. Support is done as a network or system where the responsibility for helping the novice teacher is shared by each of the participating veteran teachers. The support providers ask themselves, "How would I like to have been assisted when I was a beginning teacher?"

When I was a beginning teacher, I was pretty much on my own. Because I was hired late, and arrived close to be beginning of the school year after returning from my Peace Corps assignment in India, most of the supplies were gone, my classroom was the one in the back corner by the fire escape, and my students were the ones called "basic." The department chair acquainted me with the expected curriculum and my schedule. Fortunately, a teacher down the hall provided encouragement and let me take supplies from her stash. Otherwise, I felt quite alone.

ARC teachers can feel the same way because they are for the most part "instant teachers." It is critical that they know a support team is invested in their success. These persons need to be formally assigned to the ARC teacher at the earliest stage of the program. One of those persons who is assigned needs to be a teacher at that school site. Another person needs to be assigned from the preparation program.

Supporting new teachers must be part of the original program design. Assurances that every ARC candidate is assigned a support provider must be part of the planning and systematic decision making of the partners in an ARC program. It cannot be haphazard. It must be a specifically assigned responsibility. Support must be charted and checked. Quality ARC program support may mean a change in the way that beginning teachers are perceived. It must be a shared responsibility of all of the partners. The old African saying "It takes a village to raise a child" seems to apply here because supporting new teachers should be done with the same care as raising our children.

Developing the instructional program should also be part of the joint decision-making process. In traditional teacher preparation, the instructional process is frequently the purview of the university. The school or district involvement in teacher preparation may be little more than agreeing to take student teachers, assigning a master teacher, and attending an occasional advisory committee.

With the pressures of testing and accountability, many of the best veteran teachers are more reluctant to take on master teacher or support roles than ever before. This is not usually done from a lack of caring, but rather setting priorities when feeling overwhelmed. Districts that perceive supporting new teachers as an investment in the quality of the schools must work to assure that balance is maintained between a teacher's classroom and support responsibilities. Being a support provider must be more than just another professional obligation, and the attention placed on this role by the program partners is the first step in showing its importance and value.

ARC programs provide a natural way to change the relationship between the teacher preparation program and the school district and school. Rather than being an after-the-fact receiver of potential teachers, district personnel can become part of the preparation team. Many roles are available. At the planning level, districts can make known their needs and preferences. Asking questions such as the following can help shape the ARC program to the needs of partner districts:

Are there curriculum and schooling philosophies that the district holds that should be included in the preparation program's instructional focus?

Is there a classroom management system that should be emphasized in the preparation program?

Are there district-level initiatives that should be incorporated into the program's curriculum plan?

What facilities within the participating district can be used to make the instructional program more convenient to the candidates, more application oriented, and more connected to the day-to-day classrooms of the ARC teachers?

In many of the strongest ARC programs, the instructional program is not only jointly planned, but the classes are offered by combinations of instructors from the partners. A university professor and a teacher or principal may be co-teachers of a class. District personnel, including teachers, may be adjunct faculty at the university. Teachers and administrators may be frequent guest lecturers in the program. Both teachers and faculty may be demonstration teachers in the classrooms at the school. All of the partners may engage in action research and engage in constant discussion and reflection on practice based on watching each other work.

Because ARC candidates are teachers of record and responsible for the achievement of their students, alternative programs should take advantage of the high-stakes nature of the teaching circumstances of the ARC candidate. The performance of the candidate must be assessed regularly and systematically. Because decisions must be made for both certification and employment purposes, the best programs coordinate performance assessment and employment evaluations and make decisions jointly or in tandem with each other.

If the decisions are made based on common teaching performance expectations known to the candidate, program supervisor, evaluator from the district, and the support team, this evaluation process can be both summative and formative. The goal of any assessment system must be personal and professional growth and becoming more proficient as a teacher. There should be specific benchmarks and proficiencies to be met. All would know what they are. The process would be ongoing. There would be very few surprises.

Each of the partnering decisions just described are based on the notion that "shared power increases power." ARC programs provide an opportunity to do teacher preparation quite differently. ARC programs can change the levels of involvement of local education agencies in the preparation of teachers. ARC programs can empower local educators to be integral agents of learning to teach.

Implementing an ARC Program

Once an ARC program manager has a good idea about what kind of program the partners and participants want to put together and have developed a shared decision-making model, it is time to put the pieces together. Two concepts that should be stressed in planning and implementing an ARC program are time and data. Because ARC programs are designed to meet the immediate needs of districts, frequently there is a sense of urgency and a feeling of being behind. There will be times when this is exactly the program manager's situation. However, certain routines can be anticipated. There are elements where lead time can be built into the program implementation processes. At the same time, the strength of ARC models is the flexibility and nimbleness of the design that allows midcourse adjustments. Next are examples of program aspects that make ARC programs different from traditional programs and in my experience over the past 13 years seem to make the most difference in effective ARC programs.

Meeting District Partners' Need for Teachers

As mentioned earlier, in most well-managed districts, urban or rural, high poverty or affluent, the human resources administrators agree that they can predict to a fairly high degree of certainty how many teachers will be needed in the next school year. They have data sets that forecast trends to help them with their predictions.

If there are systems in place, such as beginning teacher induction programs, the ability to predict is even greater because retention will be greater. If teachers believe the district is invested in their success, they are much more likely to stay. If hiring practices start early and the recruiters are empowered to offer contracts in particularly hard-to-staff areas, the districts will benefit. If there is a way to track potential employees such as following graduates of the district who were in a Future Teachers of America Club through college and staying in contact with them, there is an increased chance of filling positions with persons who have a commitment to come back to the district.

As the program selects teacher candidates, the goals of the program must be kept in mind. As the program gets better known, the program will find that principals will virtually order teachers. "Can you get me another person from Troops to Teachers?" "I need a teacher for our dual-language immersion program." In teacher development, success breeds success, and employers believe that the market sensitivity and customization of the program makes it a partner with them in providing the best teachers possible for their schools.

Yet there will always have to be positions that need to be filled after the prime recruiting period. An ARC program must anticipate these occasions. Although it is not optimal, many programs set up contingencies to handle last-minute situations. Programs share candidates on rare occasions. A few teachers may be hired on temporary contracts when trend data say that positions will open up or when student census data are figured. These contingencies take trust, patience, and complete and open communication. These unknowns are the hardest part about recruitment, but calmly and deftly dealing with these late hires, including providing extra emotional and instructional support to them, is a characteristic that makes ARC programs so desirable and useful to school districts.

ARC Support Systems

Finding support providers is one of the greatest challenges for ARC programs. Not all teachers want to be support providers. Not all teachers should be support providers. Having a variety of support delivery methods and support roles should be considered. Roles vary among programs. Some programs are able to release teachers full time for a particular year and create educational roles where providing support to new and other teachers is their sole responsibility. The full-time release coaches may also serve as facilitators of the support seminars, as demonstration teachers, and as instructors of certain modules or courses. These persons are usually in these positions for a certain number of years, are selected competitively, and usually report that when they return to their classroom after their term, they are better classroom teachers themselves because of the experience.

Other support providers are involved part time to assist one or a few new teachers at their school. Other teachers want to serve in support roles but would rather be on call to assist in special subject or specialty areas. In one large urban school district that has a lot of year-round schools, providing support can be even more complicated. The district realized that the assigned support provider might not be on the same track as the new teacher. To fill that void, they created a special team of support providers called start-up coaches to provide support during the interim period until the designated support provider was available. Most of these coaches were retired teachers and administrators who were eager to serve young teachers and continue to make a contribution to the district.

Because there are so many potential responsibilities for experienced teachers, including curriculum development, serving as staff developers, acting as master teachers or induction support providers, there may not be sufficient numbers of support providers at the right sites, grades, and subjects. In these cases many ARC programs have turned to retired teachers for assistance. In many cases these retirees are eager to support new teachers. Because the support function allows more time flexibility, it is an attractive way for them to continue to be involved and serve the profession they love.

Building the cadre of support providers is a daunting task. It takes a lot of time and attention. As if finding the support providers is not enough, other aspects of building that support system must be addressed. Being a support provider requires skills that are somewhat different than regular classroom teaching skills. Training in these new skills is critical and must be planned for and executed. Record keeping of support and assistance is critical. Developing a support provider tracking system that is easy to use must be built into an ARC program's implementation plan.

In every survey I have done of ARC programs, one form of support has always been rated as the most valuable by the ARC candidates: going through the program in a cohort. Those ARC candidates that matriculate through a program as a cohort value the support they receive from each other more highly than any other kind of support. Having a group of persons with whom you share the same experiences, offer ideas when you have a problem that you could not resolve, pick you up and encourage you when you flounder, or just listen are rated as what makes the biggest difference in their becoming successful teachers. They appreciate their mentors, but they love their colleagues. Building a program that provides a reflective and systematic peer support system makes a huge difference in the long-term success of any ARC program.

Although face-to-face site-based support is the preferred method of assisting ARC candidates, program directors have used many other support methods. Even face-to-face support can take many forms. Many of the California ARC programs report that they release support providers full time to assist teaching interns. More than half of the programs release support providers for part of their work assignment. The largest type of support provided is done without release time during preparation periods, after school, in other arranged time or informally when moments can be found. In addition to site-based support, preparation programs report that the program also offers support and supervision. Programs report that the frequency varies depending on the results of the performance assessments and perceived needs as expressed by the ARC candidates, the supervisors, or the on-site support providers. There are times when there may be daily support provided. The best programs report that having some support providers who are on call to deal with difficult situations is a great asset.

Most ARC programs have embraced the notion of a broadly based support network to assist its teachers. In addition to the face-to-face support, many other modes provide support to ARC candidates. Among ways that programs have contributed to support of ARC candidates include electronic and mediated systems. Some programs have implemented hotlines. These may be phone numbers that interns can call during certain hours, or they can leave a message that will be returned, usually on the same day. Those that respond are frequently graduates of the program who find this as a way to give back to the program. Although these methods should probably not replace face-to-face support, they are one more way for beginning teachers to get the support they need.

The Internet has also been used to provide timely support. Frequently, program directors report that ARC graduates and their mentors stay in touch electronically years after they have graduated. Many programs have formal sites that the candidates can contact for immediate help. That help may include links to National Board Certified teachers or Websites about subjects or classroom resources. Some programs have set up chat rooms for their current and former ARC candidates.

The level of caring and reflection fostered by the support system has been documented in interviews and surveys of the candidates. They appreciate the care that program managers have taken to set up different ways to help them. Program managers report that these types of support do take a good deal of time and attention. These methods do not just happen. Some programs have developed alumni clubs with the express purpose of giving ARC graduates the opportunity to stay involved with the program. The graduates, more than anyone, know the value of these services, and they are eager to help when asked.

A type of support often forgotten is the special events and celebrations that many programs have developed. Three quarters of the California programs report that they include some form of year-end celebration upon graduation for their candidates. Most programs report recognition opportunities for the support providers in the program. Programs report that they have teamed with local civic organizations such as Rotary Clubs and other service organizations to offer community-based recognition and special events for ARC candidates. Some ARC programs recognize the achievements of the students of the ARC teachers. Program directors report the importance of taking every opportunity to thank those who help these programs be successful. These expressions of appreciation lead to even greater support and investment in the program.

Delivering Instruction in an ARC Program

Another characteristic of ARC programs is the range of delivery patterns in the instructional system. Managing a program that adjusts the instructional program to the needs of the clients, yet adheres to the standards and expectations of the state certification agency, is another area for consideration and attention. Most of those who strongly advocate ARC affirm the importance of meeting the same standards as all other forms of teacher preparation. Where they differ is in their commitment to adjusting the model as necessary to accommodate the needs of the clients—the districts and ARC teachers. Among the examples of possible adjustments in the instructional program are the following examples.

Dividing instruction into smaller segments such as modules rather than teaching courses in traditional three-semester unit segments is a frequent modification in ARC programs. This allows instruction to be offered when it is likely to have the greatest impact—just before the skill, knowledge, or ability is to be applied. Modularized coursework also allows the curriculum to be spiraled and to move from foundational knowledge to more sophisticated skills in the program.

For example, in reading skills, there are skills that the teacher must have before entering the classroom, such as foundational phonemic skills. But there are others, such as diagnosing phonemic errors, that are likely to be learned more powerfully as the teacher is applying those skills with the students. In the area of classroom management, instruction that accompanies application allows for adjustments to be made in the curriculum and in its application. In an ARC program course, instructors need to be agile enough to stop and reteach when students are having difficulty with the application of a particular concept. Having classes offered when the teachers are practicing the skills and strategies allows the connection of theory and practice that connects both and makes what is learned more powerful. Instructors who exhibit the flexibility to adjust their plans in the learning-by-doing mode will result in far more permanent learning by the ARC candidates.

Instruction that is spiraled, segmented, and situational are hallmarks of excellent ARC programs. The context that the ARC teacher is experiencing does matter. Having an instructional and support program that accounts for the circumstances the ARC teachers are experiencing makes the learning experience as powerful as any that educators have conceived. Pragmatic learning works. This is particularly true when this learning is accompanied by the theoretical constructs that show why it can work and the impediments that may cause it to fail. Frequently it is the other ARC students in the class who help provide context for this instruction.

When a program is purposely planned to link instruction, support, and assessment of performance, the probability of useful, lasting learning is immense. If instruction and performance assessment are based on the same skills and expectations, and there are opportunities to teach and reteach the concepts, the result will be the kinds of applied learning recognized by cognitive psychologists as the most powerful instruction that leads to lasting and reflective learning.

In addition to the types of instructional delivery just listed, many programs have, by necessity, resorted to other delivery modes to accommodate candidates in the program. For example, most of the programs that serve remote areas use mediated communication, including the Internet, interactive television, and other distance learning services. Many programs report that the use of distance technology requires certain attributes that may not be as necessary as more traditional delivery. In addition to technological skills, these technologies require levels of independence and persistence that may not be necessary when the instruction is face to face. Distance programs have also reported that the support system becomes even more important to combat the feeling of isolation on the part of candidates.

Data-Driven Decision Making and Program Evaluation

Every decision made in an ARC program should be, at least in part, based on the data that the program has collected. From initial application to the program to following the ARC graduates, data need to be collected to determine if the program is achieving its goals and reaching its potential. Another reason why data are collected is to help directors tell the story of the program. In most states ARC is authorized by specific legislative authorization. Those who enacted the legislation are likely to want to know if the program is accomplishing what was intended. Just as assessment procedures are used to promote candidate growth and learning, every program evaluation should have as its goal to improve program effectiveness.

Among the types of data that should be collected are demographic data about the participants. This includes data about what, if any, careers the candidates had before choosing to enter teaching. Data that can be used for program improvement include information about the support system, including visitation records, data about the frequency of instructional concerns that participants raise that could inform the program about what needs to be emphasized or retaught, and satisfaction with the system by the ARC candidate. Included within descriptive data would be the types of support offered, the persons who provide support, and the frequency of the interactions. For example, many programs have turned to Web-based support or hotlines to supplement face-to-face support. The effectiveness of each of these types of support should be measured.

Whenever data are collected, those surveyed should receive summary information. Those who take the time to answer questions are usually interested in the results. They would also be interested to hear reports of how the data were used, and they are more likely to complete the next survey if they have seen results of the last one. Treating candidates, support providers, and other partners as valued participants and affirming their role in program improvement benefits everyone.

Data collection and presentation make an ARC program come alive. In addition to quantitative data, other kinds of data can also be powerful. All data must reference back to the goals of the ARC program. All data must respond to the inquiries of the program's partners and constituencies. These constituencies include the graduates of the program, those who hire them, and the state agencies and legislature that enabled the program to begin.

One form of data often overlooked is the experiential reflections of those who manage ARC programs. These reflections when gathered around particular themes become important diagnostic tools because they point out trends that help new program directors and can be very instructive as programs and policy makers determine the lessons of ARC programs. As much as I love quantitative data, the stories that ARC candidates tell are the ones that have had the most lasting effect on me. Their words make the program more real. Their words speak to those things that are really important. Although these data may not be statistically reliable or even replicable, if we listen, the richness of the experience will be exposed or the places where we need to get better will be revealed.

Conclusion

Twenty-plus years of experience with alternative routes to certification in California have led to a number of insights about what is possible in this type of teacher preparation. Not all of these insights will be transferable. ARC programs have been particularly fortunate for the past 13 years because the state budget of California has provided funding for ARC. I hope that some of our experiences are useful to those who are developing or expanding their programs and our lessons will help program directors not make the mistakes we have made.

In this chapter I have provided examples of areas that are likely to lead to successful ARC programs. These are the areas that must receive attention as managers develop and implement an ARC program. The first task is to establish the goals of the program, which should be based on an extensive needs analysis of your clients—the districts in your service area and the potential teachers for your program.

Part of setting goals and developing the mission statement is understanding the limits and potential traps associated with ARC programs. ARC should not be seen as a replacement for more traditional forms of teacher preparation. ARC has a special niche, and the program should find that place based on the needs of the service area. Among the traps that ARC can fall into is viewing programs as easier routes. If ARC programs do not adhere to the same standards as other state certification programs, they will not be able to stand the tests of time and will eventually fade.

One of the program aspects that allows program flexibility is that ARC programs do not have to provide a full range of preparation or certification options. If there are sufficient numbers of social science or physical education teachers, then those programs should not be offered. If the need for elementary teachers drops, as it has in California, programs need to be flexible enough to shift emphasis to those areas where the demand is greater, such as special education. ARC programs are not for all teacher candidates. They are generally not well suited for potential teachers with relatively little work experience. The graduated experiences of a student teaching–based program are likely to be a more appropriate model. For those who come to teaching with a desire to teach and a background in experience-based learning, ARC programs are more likely to fit their adult learning style.

Another reason why ARC has become an important teacher preparation option is that the model may be more adaptable than more traditional teacher preparation. Instruction can be delivered in many different formats and be offered at sites that are more attractive and adjacent to the teacher's worksite. Instruction can be adjusted to the needs of the ARC candidates, and midcourse corrections are the norm rather than an exception.

Immediacy, practicality, and application of skills and abilities are the bedrock of the program. The support, instruction, and performance assessment systems must be linked, aligned, and inform each other.

ARC programs encourage active participation of all educators in teacher preparation. Unless programs are collaborative and participatory, there is far less reason for the program to exist. ARC programs are built on the importance of encouraging the formal participation of experienced practitioners in developing novice teachers.

Many of the practices and lessons described in this chapter are also characteristics of any high-quality teacher preparation program. Many believe that the existence of ARC programs has led more traditional programs to modify their practices and become more field based and more sensitive to the needs of districts. That may be the most positive result of ARC. If programs and their partners are looking for a way to expand the talent pool of teachers and bring into teaching those who might not be able to fulfill their desire to teach, then ARC is well suited to this goal. If those interested in teacher preparation want to develop a program that connects the theoretical and the practical on a daily basis and offers an instructional program where experienced practitioners lead in the development of novice teachers, ARC can provide this.

To be successful and sustainable, ARC programs must be part of the broader context of teacher preparation. It must be a route to certification, not an alternative with separate rules and standards. In ARC programs it is important that policymakers, program directors, and their district-level partners perceive teacher preparation as an investment in the partnering districts' future and put the resources in place to fund that investment. The ultimate goal of any ARC program is to improve the educational performance of students of the ARC candidates through improved preparation, support, and assistance of these new teachers. Anything less is not worth the effort.

INDEX

Appraise
Caliber
Maverick
referendum
redundant